I read *In A Sun-Scorched Land* in one sitting, laughing, crying, and cheering for the Ebenhack family as God knit them together in a most extraordinary way. You don't want to miss this book. It will strengthen your faith and remind you that God is at work in the details of our lives every day.

—GILLIAN MARCHENKO
Author of *Sun Shine Down* and *Still Life*

I often ask the Lord for perspective, and sometimes He answers in a way that takes my breath away. Jen's book was an exhilarating answer to that prayer. I read *In a Sun-Scorched Land* during a challenging season and a particularly rough week. Her story brought clarity and focus, reminding me of how blessed I am and how faithful God is. The shift in perspective was a gift in itself, but so was the enjoyment I received from a thrilling story, skillfully told. This is a modern-day missionary adventure story that will keep you on the edge of your seat while strengthening your faith.

—TRINA HOLDEN
Author of *Your Real Food Journey*, Blogger at TrinaHolden.com

Jennifer has written the story of God's redemptive and powerful work in her family's journey toward adoption. Her faith, strengthened by years of struggle and pain in the country of Haiti, relentlessly pursued the heart of Jesus—no matter her circumstance. This book will inspire your heart to never give up on the things (and people!) the Lord has called you to, as well as reveal the gifts that are ours when we wait on the Lord and walk in His grace.

—JULIE BRASINGTON
Blogger at HappyHomeFairy.com

# In a SUN-SCORCHED Land

A memoir of adoption, faith, and the moving of Haiti's mountains

# JENNIFER EBENHACK

LOYAL
ARTS MEDIA

Published by Loyal Arts Media
P.O. Box 1414
Bend, OR 97709
loyalartsmedia.com

Printed in the United States of America

Cover design by Rebecca Finch
Cover photo by Michelle Matthews

ISBN 978-1-929125-35-7 (paperback)

I dedicate this book to four generations of "earthen vessels," my family members who know the pain of brokenness, yet use their cracks and scars to shine Christ's light to the world around them:

First to Virgil and Phyllis Litke, my grandparents, who have provided an example of godliness and faith through all of life's trials. *Thank you for the legacy you provide for the generations to come.*

Secondly, to Brenda Jordan, my mother, whose dependence on Jesus turns deserts into springs. *Thank you for showing me that the joy of the Lord is our strength.*

Thirdly, to Jarod, my husband, whose love has never faltered despite the very worst of conditions. *Thank you for protecting and cherishing me through better, worse, richer, poorer, in sickness and in health.*

And finally, to Justin, Jaden, and Daphne, who already know the bitterness of life in this fallen world, yet are also learning at a young age the power of redemption, and to Dora and Brendan whose sensitive hearts are poised and ready to pour out God's love. *I pray each of you will trust Jesus, not only with your eternity as you've already done, but also with every moment of your life. He has a beautiful plan for every single one of you.*

# Table of Contents

# Foreword

Some stories are just too good to be true.

Others are too tragic to even fathom.

But some stories . . . *some* stories are such an incredible mix of hard and raw and beautiful that they can only come from God.

And that would be the kind of story behind Jennifer Ebenhack's memoir. A gripping, heart-breaking, hope-filled story of love and sacrifice that somehow miraculously swirls together on the sun-scorched sands of Haiti. Hers is a story which shows the journey of an ordinary woman on the road from the impossible to the possible. And for this reason, it is a story we all should read and know.

Most of us will never wake up and find ourselves on a dirt road in the middle of Haiti and not everyone will embark on that difficult and loving path toward adopting children. But who doesn't know what it's like to hit rock bottom? To stumble, struggle, and question how you ever got there in the first place?

In so many ways—in our different lives and different homes—we are all like Jennifer, a woman at the end of her rope. Choking, slipping, grasping, drowning. And when we're in the middle of our impossible, we need to hear of those who have gone before.

And that's what I loved and appreciated about Jennifer's story: how it put my impossible into perspective. You can picture her husband bravely facing invading criminals with nothing but pepper-spray and a baseball bat. You can hear the dogs barking their warning and grieve over her children's scared and lonely cries. You can also feel the pain of a mother's heart breaking over and over again with one disappointment after another.

But as Jennifer's story unfolds, you will never doubt that God is with her every step of the way. You will see Him working, even when she can't. You might well find yourself cheering for her and whispering, *Don't give up and don't lose hope. Keep your faith, no matter what happens.*

Although it may seem like too many hardships.

Too many defeats. Too many things gone wrong.

*Impossible.*

And yet, we hang on to this strange hope because we serve a God who works wonders far beyond anything we can imagine.

He is a God of miracles who specializes in the impossible.

My friend, are you looking for renewed hope and beautiful inspiration? If so, get ready to be deeply touched by Jennifer's amazing story; not because she is such a heroic figure and wonderful person (although I'd say she is both) but because our God is an impossible God.

Yes, He really can move mountains.

-LISA JACOBSON
CLUB31WOMEN.COM

# A Note to the Reader

This story involves a lot of people, none of them perfect. Some walked in complete rebellion to God's will, and others loved him dearly, yet made decisions they later regretted, as we all do from time to time. As I share the experiences of my family and the ministries and country in which we worked, I ask that you give grace. I tell our story as factually as possible, but my goal is never to incriminate or condemn. Our enemy has never been "flesh and blood" but rather "the cosmic powers over this present darkness," and "the spiritual forces of evil in the heavenly places" (Ephesians 6:12). Though the broken relationships in this book have already been restored, I have changed names to protect the privacy of a number of individuals.

# Introduction

I had to have seen the sight a million times those eight years in Haiti: the *taptap*–the trucks, vans, and pickups used for public transportation–bearing more bodies than my North American mind could comprehend. Seeing it is one thing–the bottom of the vehicle scraping the ground at each bump, the brakes squealing, the engine grinding, the gears clashing. The lifespan of a vehicle-turned-taptap has to be less than five years, though some spit, welding, and duct tape can grant them a little extra life. Yeah, seeing it is crazy. But riding a taptap is another experience altogether. Because when you're crammed so far into the lap of the person beside you that you know what they last ate and when they last bathed, you don't believe the driver would dare pick up another traveler. But of course, he does. To him, another body is a few more *gourdes* in his pocket. Sure the vehicle is closer to dying by the minute, but in Haiti, life is lived for today. There's no guarantee you'll even be around tomorrow–that's how hard things are–so forget about keeping your vehicle in good shape, cram another person inside and put a few more grains of rice on the table tonight.

All too often, life feels like one of those rides. And we wonder if our Driver is mindless of the load, ignorant to our discomfort or simply unconcerned with our well-being. *Doesn't He see? Doesn't He care? There has to be a limit to what we can bear! Why doesn't He do something?*

In Haiti, I felt I'd scraped bottom. Not only was life too hard to handle, but I was also faced with my own sinfulness. I'd have done almost anything to escape, anything to make the pain go away. Some days it was a dull ache, a mild depression. But some days the feelings hit sharp and hard, and I was blinded by anxiety and desperation.

Even back in the comfort and supposed safety of the States, when the physical traumas had passed, when Haiti's earthquake was over, adrenal fatigue left me imprisoned by fear. On one of the worst days, my eyes fell on a plaque in our temporary housing unit: "The LORD will guide you always; he will satisfy your needs . . . and will strengthen your frame" (Isaiah 58:11 NIV).

I looked it up. Isaiah 58:10–11 provided more context:

And if you spend yourselves in behalf of the hungry
    and satisfy the needs of the oppressed,
then your light will rise in the darkness,
    and your night will become like the noonday.
The LORD will guide you always;
    he will satisfy your needs in a sun-scorched land
    and will strengthen your frame.
You will be like a well-watered garden,
    like a spring whose waters never fail.

The verses captivated me. For eight years I'd lived in a sun-scorched land, ministering, mothering, and fighting adoption battles on behalf of three abandoned children. For eight years I'd spent myself on behalf of the hungry and oppressed. For eight years I'd been the taptap, carrying heavier loads than I'd thought possible, yet amazingly, finding God's mercies to be new every morning. But on this day, in the serenity of Kansas, my mind, body, and spirit continued paying the price for all I'd given, and the lies of fatigue and anxiety taunted. *Accept it: It was too much for you. You're used up. Alone.*

But here in Isaiah 58 was hope. The reminder that the dry and used-up can always be transformed, strengthened.

That hope would see me through the dark days ahead. For it was the hope I'd already known. It lifted my eyes above all that took place on the dust-engulfed Haitian roads; taking my gaze to the hills, to the turquoise waters on Haiti's northern shores, to the palm branches rustling in sea breezes, to the bold blue skies with crisp white clouds. That hope had always been my life-line. And the more I would reflect on the grace I'd experienced in yesterday's heat, the more healing I would know.

I'm past those deserts. In their places are springs. His promises were true. But that doesn't mean the end of difficulty. Today's burdens are in a different land, in different contexts, but they're always tempered by hope. Not mere optimism, but rather a calm confidence and assurance. This hope I cling to is based on fact: the fact that my God and Creator wants a personal relationship with me, the fact that He's divinely orchestrating my entire life to prove His relentless love, the fact that He's trustworthy and good, the fact that there's a glorious ending to my story—or really, a glorious beginning, when I will shake off the brokenness of this life and trade it in for eternity with Jesus, my Savior.

If you are tired, weary, or broken in any way, I've written my story for you. May God use it to lift your eyes to blue skies and crystal waters even while you swelter in this sun-scorched land. Know this: He will guide you. He will satisfy your needs, even here in the heat. He will strengthen your frame. As you cling to Him, He'll take the desert life you're living and turn it into a well-watered garden, a spring whose waters never fail. Not only will He help you, my friend, He'll turn you into an oasis for others who are parched.

This is part of my story—a crazy-dramatic season of adventure I didn't realize I'd signed up for. But more than that, it's God's story, the kind He delights to write in the lives of all His children. The kind in which He works again and again, under the scorching sun, breathing life and restoring hope.

I pray by the end, your confidence will be firm; you'll see He's in complete control. He is the hope in *your* sun-scorched land as well.

# Prologue

Cape Haitian, Haiti

*Jesus, help.* It was the most eloquent prayer I could manage.

"Jen!" Jarod whispered. "I'm going to wake Sarah!"

Fear had been no stranger the past four years in Haiti, but this . . . this was terror. A gang of criminals had scaled the wall and dropped into our backyard. A thousand desperate thoughts flooded into my head. I'd professed faith for over two decades, but this night moved trust past theory, past churchy conversations.

I changed out of my pajamas while Jarod raced down the tiled stairs to our intern's apartment. Moments later, Sarah scrambled up the stairs, followed by Jarod, who toted a five-gallon jug of gasoline he'd snatched from the porch.

Jarod padlocked and dead-bolted the metal door between the stairs and our entryway.

"What about the kids? Should I bring them to our room?" I was trembling, longing to gather and protect my brood—the five munchkins I'd been exasperated with only a few hours before.

"I don't think we should." Jarod kept his voice low. His steadiness surprised me. "Better for them to sleep and know nothing."

17

*Know what?* I wondered. *How will this end?*

Sarah and I followed Jarod back into the shadows of the bedroom. His voice, directed through the open window slats, startled me: "What do you want?"

"We want your money," came the bold reply from below. No doubt the man's confidence came from the cover of darkness and, more significantly, the protective blessing of a voodoo priest.

Other members of the gang fanned out, looking for points of entry.

"We keep our money at the bank." Jarod kept the Creole conversation going to buy time. "Do you think we're crazy enough to keep money on hand for thieves?"

Either they were counting on such foolishness or they had other things in mind. Stories of their violence—stories I couldn't stomach—circled the neighborhood. *Jesus, we need you. We have nothing—no emergency responders, no weapons, nothing.*

The three of us jumped at the sound of a rattling balcony door only a few feet away, and my heart leapt for my baby on the other side of that wall, my five-month-old boy, asleep under his mosquito net. *Protect him, Jesus,* I cried silently. *Let him sleep.*

Jarod flew into action. He grabbed a box of matches and the jug of gas and whispered instructions. "Lock yourselves in the bathroom and call for help. Call the Froeses. Call anyone. We need someone to scare these guys away or help us catch them." Clinging to each other, Sarah and I complied, and Jarod crept to the doorway. Maneuvering the jug's spigot, he managed to pour a stream of gas under the balcony door.

Again his voice broke the silence: "Do you want to burn?" He held a match, ready to light the oily puddle if necessary. The door stopped shaking and the man jumped down.

From the safety of the ground, the thief gave full vent to his anger. "Ma fize-w!" *I'll shoot you!*

"Go ahead." Jarod fought to keep his voice calm. "Your feet are already soaked in gasoline. Pull the trigger and you'll catch fire."

There was no shot. Just another threat: "We'll kill you when we get in!"

I rejoined Jarod in the hall as glass crashed beneath us.

"Sarah's windows," he muttered. "That means they're inside."

We could hear them pillaging through her things, and I couldn't help but wonder what would've happened if she was still there.

"Is anyone coming to help?" Jarod asked.

"Tom is on his way. He's bringing spotlights." I paused to listen to the voices downstairs. "Sarah's door is locked, right?"

"It's padlocked, but I couldn't find the key for the dead-bolt." He didn't sound as confident as I wanted him to be.

"How bad is that?"

"We've only got a few more seconds."

I felt the blood drain from my face.

Jarod pressed his ear against the metal door at the top of our stairway—the final barrier between us and the gang. *Was our safety really resting on a sheet of metal an eighth of an inch thick?*

He listened, and I studied the door's ventilation shafts, twelve inches tall, right about head level, with space enough for a gun-wielding hand to reach through.

The door below rattled. Jarod, dripping with sweat, positioned himself with the gas can again. His readiness did nothing to ease my panic. There was no plan B. No time for instructions if plan A failed. We'd fight, yes, but we were unarmed and outnumbered.

*Trust.*

The concept felt so risky. There was no control in trust. Could I? Would I?

I'd thought myself so daring to embark on this journey into international adoption and cross-cultural ministry. I'd begun to trust three decades earlier as a child, and I thought I'd long ago passed the course. But tonight proved otherwise. And with this new test thrust upon me, there'd been no time to review my notes. I had front-row seating to a David-versus-Goliath fight, with my family as the plunder.

How was I to trust, when my own hands were empty, even of a sling and stone?

I heard the clank of metal. "Jarod! Did they break through?"

The footsteps on the stairs answered my question.

# 1

## Day One

If I take the wings of the morning
and dwell in the uttermost parts of the sea,
even there your hand shall lead me,
and your right hand shall hold me.

Psalm 139:9–10

AUGUST 15, 2002

As our wheels bounced down onto the Port-au-Prince runway, I wasn't sure if I should attribute my pounding heart and sweaty palms to elation or fear. We skidded to a stop, not too far from a goat, and it was official: Jarod and I were in Haiti to stay—cause for emotions of all varieties. The deepest yearnings of my heart were about to be fulfilled, while I simultaneously felt I was entering Mordor from the *Lord of the Rings*. Jarod squeezed my hand, undoubtedly processing similar thoughts, and I peered through the scratched plexiglass window. The sunshine and palm trees advertised paradise, but I knew better. Banana-leaf shanties and voodoo flags beneath the palms told the truer story: Paradise lost, a tragic cliché.

Flight attendants instructed us in Creole, French, and English. The handful of white passengers pulled on their backpacks, while the Haitians composing the rest of the planeload gathered arms full of American bounty—primarily boom boxes and hats—to share with friends and relatives. The doors finally opened, and Jarod and I, sans extravagant gifts, left the first-world comfort of air-conditioning behind. Our gift, we hoped, was a lifetime of service. But as the heat knocked the breath right out of us, my flesh faltered for a moment. Jarod heard me gasp. "We'll get used to it," he reassured me, and I hoped he was right. I was here to make a difference though, and really, nothing less than an act of force could have kept me from moving forward.

We descended the stairs to the tarmac, then snaked our way behind the others to the terminal building. As I clasped Jarod's hand, my heart soared. I'd dreamed of serving God internationally my whole life, and here I was. We would minister full-time with Truth in Haiti, a Canada-based organization whose forms of outreach included church ministry, an orphanage, and adoptions. Jarod would serve as the mission's first in-country administrator, responsible to TIH's North American founder and president, Mark Riley. I would help wherever I could in addition to managing our rented home, across the street from TIH's orphanage.

But following the passion of our hearts into mission work wasn't all that brought us here. In addition to birthing our ministry career, we were birthing a family—*today*. This was the day our three-year dream of becoming parents would be realized. There would be no party, no fanfare, no grandparents around to ooh and aah, just the act of bringing twin toddlers—Justin and Jaden—out of TIH's orphanage into our home. We'd begun their adoption paperwork in January of 2001, under the impression that they could be whisked to Chicago in a few short months. But today, a year and a half later, it was Jarod and I who were transplanted. The past eighteen months had been filled with frustrations and delays—a labor that still hadn't borne any children. But before the sun set, my aching empty arms would engulf my babies. Now that we were here, surely the delivery—their official adoption—couldn't be long in coming.

We reached the entrance to Mais Gate International Airport, an open-air passageway that smelled of hot cement and well-warmed, garlic-infused bodies. With even less enthusiasm than the stereotypical airport employee, immigration officials stamped our passports, unceremoniously plunking our root systems into pots of unfamiliar soil. We stepped a few feet forward, past what our noses informed us were the public restrooms, into the baggage claim. Waiting for us, under fluorescent lights and ceiling fans, was Anderson, the TIH driver and mechanic, reasonably fluent in English. After the customary two-cheek kiss, we all exited the airport. Even under Anderson's care, we couldn't avoid being mobbed by taxi drivers and baggage handlers, eager for a few American dollars in exchange for a service. We shouldered our way through the intense crowd, declining offers to help us do what we were successfully managing already. Two lessons I'd learned from previous visits came back to me quickly: (1) eye contact is an invitation to engage, and (2) inhaling in the presence of so many sweaty men is risky business.

As we loaded the SUV in the airport parking lot, someone must have sounded the foreigner alarm. Cries of "*Blan! Blan!*" rang out from more than one direction. A dirty child holding a baby hurried toward me at her mother's urging. "*Blan!* Geeve me won dollah!" A man with a crutch limped his way across the pavement, his cup of coins jingling as he too demanded a dollar. My heart fell. Jarod and I were no strangers to such pleas, having spent the past several years in urban Chicago, where homeless people abounded; yet Haiti presented such a baffling new level of poverty and dependence that I felt as helpless as the beggars. The words "sorry, not today" rolled easily off my lips on Chicago streets, but now as I fumbled a few similar words in Creole, my heart yearned for the ability to explain, to understand, to provide the answer. *I can't just give you money, little girl, sir. I'm here to help. I'm here to raise two boys and help as many as I can. I don't know what to do for you today. But I care. I care more than "one dollar."*

But before those thoughts could reach my tangled tongue, Anderson started the engine and drove away, and any thoughts whatsoever flew out the window as I concentrated simply on remaining upright. The streets were so bad, we may as well have been off-roading. Anderson swerved to avoid potholes and honked to alert pedestrians, who jumped to the side and yanked children out of our path. I wondered if the speedometer was working properly. Could we only be going forty-five miles per hour?

Jarod gripped the handle above the front passenger seat to stabilize himself and made small talk with Anderson. I "enculturated" myself by looking out the window. The taptaps came in all forms: cars, pickups, vans, and school buses, operating as privately owned "public" transportation. Every square inch of them was covered in Caribbean colors, with hand-painted pictures of anything under the sun. One bus featured Jesus' face, Michael Jordan, an airplane, a Nike swoosh, and the phrase "I love you, Baby." Most prominently displayed on each was a Bible verse reference and biblical name. *How ironic that we're missionaries to a culture that looks so blatantly Christian.* But we would soon learn that this was born of Catholic and voodoo superstition. There was much more to Haiti than met the eye. Many of the innumerable Christians who sang out praises in church on Sundays would be visiting their witch doctor on Monday.

I studied the people a mere arm's length from my window, intrigued by their dress. Similar to the taptaps, people wore outfits of unexpected color and pattern combinations. There was no native dress here, as in Africa or India, yet there was still a distinctive Haitian look. Or maybe there were many Haitian looks. I spotted a teenager frilled and ruffled in a dress that I would have deemed appropriate only for a five-year-old, and beside her some women in their twenties sported trendy denim skirts and tight-knit tops. But most grown women wore any manner of wild combinations—flowered skirts together with striped tops, pink jumpers paired with red blouses—oblivious to any fashion faux paus they might be committing. Besides, they had more serious matters on their minds. Literally. Atop their heads they carried weighty loads from the small to the impossibly large: a five-gallon bucket full of water, a plastic tub full of live chickens, a gallon jug of oil, a dozen flats of eggs. A few of them used one arm to steady their load.

There weren't quite as many men in action, though nearly all the vehicles were driven by males. Other men muscled wheelbarrow loads to the market, shirtless, barefoot, and glossed with sweat. Some sat by the road, playing games. I did a double-take at the sight of clothespins clipped around the perimeter of one man's face.

"What is *that* about?"

"He's losing the card game," Jarod answered. He'd asked Pastor Mark the same question on a previous trip. "They bet pain instead of money and clip on another clothespin each time they lose."

"I think we're almost there now," Jarod said, leaning forward. Everything looked the same to me, but I was learning to trust his internal GPS. I wished I'd been born with one too, as my navigational skills were somewhat less than flawless.

We turned off the road unaptly named a highway, and as our tires fought the rocky incline, my heart danced. *Almost there!* I looked out my window through a swirl of dust, and spotted it—a blue cement-block house, the words *Krech Verite en Ayiti*—Truth in Haiti Orphanage—sketched in black paint across the front. *I'm coming, boys!* Justin and Jaden weren't legally ours yet, but since we were here as TIH employees, we were allowed to take custody of them as soon as we were ready.

We made our final turn onto *Impasse Jean*, the dead-end street to our walled-in house. Anderson honked, and Jamison, our newly employed guard, opened the black iron gate, beaming in our direction. He had reason beyond friendliness to smile. Hiring him as our guard and groundskeeper for $200 per month made him a wealthy man by Haitian standards. He would stay in the *dependans*, the extra rooms that the nicer Haitian homes featured for hired help, but he'd receive time off each week to spend back home with his wife and two young children. Though we felt bad separating the family at all, everyone with TIH assured us that this was completely appropriate in Haiti—a privilege, rather than an inconvenience. I didn't like it, but figured that as newcomers we should defer to their judgment.

While the men unloaded the SUV, I toured our home—the first actual house of our married life. Up until now, Jarod and I had lived in a dormitory apartment. Now we had three bedrooms, two baths, a living room, kitchen, and office. Jamison's room and the laundry room were accessible only from the outside.

The house was not impressive by American standards. It was hot, dark, and a bit cramped despite the number of rooms it boasted. There were termite trails through the wooden doorframes and cracks adorning the cement walls and ceiling. The iron security bars on the windows—a feature we would learn more about in the coming years—alerted the discerning viewer to the risks of the neighborhood. But Jarod and I were endeavoring to see things through Haitian eyes, counting ourselves fortunate indeed to have a roof over our heads, a tiled floor beneath us, bug spray for the pests, and thankfully, no history of crack-disturbing earthquakes in the area. While I remained apprehensive about my ability to handle some elements of my new home—heat and cockroaches especially—I couldn't help but remember the attractive furnishings I'd brought with me. Even the Walmart bedspreads and cheap little throw rugs would have been beyond the budget of those around us. I wondered if I'd ever be able to reconcile the two opposing worlds of which I was now a part. *How does a woman who has never missed a meal in her life relate to the starving?*

My thoughts bounced back to our boys, who were only steps away. The orphanage drew me like a magnet, but the moment was too holy to experience alone. I'd wait for Jarod. What was another fifteen minutes after a year and a half?

As I walked through the house, my thoughts drifted back over the past eighteen months. I'd worked for these boys who had captured my heart. Sheer force of will took me through thousands of legal processes in record time. I designed adoption announcements. I remodeled a bedroom on a budget. I gave inspirational speeches to anyone curious about adoption. And I prayed, frustrated and broken when my strivings failed to speed things along. I cried out to God from the spotless nursery. *Don't you know how badly our boys need us? I know you see them—alone in an institution, already learning, knowing things aren't as they should be. Don't you realize every day counts? If babies in the womb need their mother's voice and love, how much more these toddlers, already abandoned, already scarred? Here we are, God, ready to step in. We volunteered for this job—isn't that what you wanted? Can't you just bring them home?*

In November of 2001, Jarod and I canceled a once-in-a-lifetime vacation to Mexico due to a rumor that the process was near completion. In December, I displayed our mini plastic evergreen above the reach of toddler hands, ever hopeful of a Christmas miracle. In January, I boxed the tree up, mournful there had been no danger at all of ornament-breaking disasters. The wait that was such a trial was only the prelude to life in Haiti, where things would seldom, if ever, go as planned.

But the wait was imperative. We had to be stilled to be redirected.

We'd been confident of God's plan: we were to serve Him in Papua New Guinea. But then through the adoption process, the things we'd been most certain of were turned upside down. Our hearts were stirred to join Truth in Haiti, and we decided to make a trip. Maybe a step of faith in this new direction would clarify things.

Of course the most thrilling part of that visit was meeting Justin and Jaden. In the dark heat, only hours after entering the country that first time, we were introduced to our sons. Justin seemed mortified to meet us. In a photograph of that incredible moment, I am the picture of joy and he of abject misery. As for Jaden, well, Jaden gave the phrase "out of control" deep new meaning. We had known he had a lazy eye, but we hadn't known about his crippled left arm, nor—slightly more significantly—his special needs. After he'd been in Jarod's arms for an entire two seconds, we knew we were destined for exhaustion. If I'd ever met a child whose behavior could accurately be compared to the infamous "Taz" of the Looney Tunes world, this was him.

Though we were only visiting, we were allowed to take the boys out of the orphanage and bring them to the team accommodations. We jumped at the chance to bond as a family for a few days and then paid dearly for our decision. Jaden ran, jumped, spun, flung, writhed, and flopped for the next few hours. *At least he'll be worn out by bedtime,* I thought.

Had Jarod and I been the sole occupants of our king-sized bed that night, sleep would have been elusive enough due to oppressive heat, street dogfights, and the endless crowing of roosters. But it wasn't just Jarod and me in the bed; it was the whole family. Little had I known that it was entirely possible to wiggle, bounce, fling, writhe, and flop all night as well. I checked my watch hour after hour.

2:00 a.m. Marvel at Jaden's ability to endlessly thump his torso on the mattress.

3:00 a.m. Balance on the bed's edge to avoid being kicked.

4:00 a.m. Mop the sweat from my face, listen to another dogfight.

5:00 a.m. Push Jaden's feet out of my face, give up on sleep.

Jarod was equally "refreshed." Through bleary eyes, we watched our boys stir out of their sleep, full of boundless energy for the new day.

About forty-eight hours into that initial tour d'Haiti, I was as overwhelmed by the country itself as I was by our boys. My weaknesses glared like the Haitian sun, and I wasn't at all sure that I was cut out for the things that had looked so glamorous from afar. But a few days, more than a few tears, and one serious wrestling match with God later, I was ready to limp forward.

Maybe limping was all God wanted from me.

I heard Anderson drive off our yard, and I snapped back to the present. Today the waiting was over. We were here to stay; we were a family in Haiti for all practical purposes, even if we couldn't yet travel to the States together.

"Jen! You ready?" Jarod burst through the open bedroom door. He was already stained with sweat and like me should have been exhausted from the past days leading up to our move, but his excitement to claim our sons buoyed him up and put a sparkle in his eyes.

"Absolutely!" I jumped up and took his outstretched hand. Our hurried steps marked the final minutes of our three years alone together. But there was no holding us back.

We rapped the metal orphanage gate with a stone in order to be heard above the noise of the thirty-some kids inside. The orphanage guard opened the door, greeting us respectfully, aware that the pale individuals before him were the new missionaries. I knew he didn't carry a weapon like the guards at Haitian banks, but I was still reassured by the idea of someone keeping watch. I eyed the nine-foot-high cement wall, topped with pieces of broken glass, grateful for the added security it provided. Little did I know how false that sense of security would prove to be in our own yard in the coming days.

We made our way over the hot cement to the orphanage entrance. The building was a two-story block house with staircases, doorways, and levels in the oddest of places. That was the norm in Haitian construction—not a lot of forethought, just rooms, stairs, plumbing, and wiring added as needed.

We entered the barred-in porch, eagerly scanning it for our

boys. Not seeing them, we continued inside, pausing to let our eyes adjust to the dim light. The TIH orphanage was relatively organized, but without reliable electricity, running water, functional toilets, or even an indoor kitchen. It was sometimes hard to believe that the children inside were better off than most in Haiti. I took it all in again—smudged walls, mismatched clothes, bare feet, runny noses.

"There they are!" Jarod pointed, and my pulse quickened. I would remember this forever—these last few moments they belonged to the orphanage. Their oversized T-shirts hung on them like dresses. Jaden was spinning in circles, and Justin was chatting with a fellow two-year-old. But to my delight, they came running the second they spied us. Justin wrapped his wiry arms around my neck as I scooped him up, and my heart melted. Of course, the ninety-degree room was melting the rest of me as well, but in my joy I had no thought of the heat. Jarod snagged Jaden, who eyed his new daddy with fascination—turning back and forth, alternating between his strong and lazy eye like a curious brown-eyed bird.

As we carried our boys out into the sunshine, we spoke and smiled our gratitude to those who had done the most with our sons. Some of them would be sad to lose their wards, but they also knew we'd be just across the street, and they'd be seeing Richard and Butah again.

The boys' names were a bit of an issue; their birth mother had named them Richard and Richardo, and for a while the orphanage workers dubbed Richardo "Cargo." Then, when he began obsessively using the nonsense word *butah*, the orphanage staff adopted that as his nickname. We decided we'd keep Richard and Richardo as middle names, but we'd taken special care as we chose their new first names about a year earlier. Justin, meaning "just one," was assigned to Richard; and Jaden, a name from the Bible meaning "God has heard," replaced Richardo, Cargo, and the ever-so-dignified Butah.

After a simple goodbye to the orphanage caregivers, the boys were in our custody. They warmed quickly to their new home across the street. It felt like Christmas morning as Jarod and I pointed out their beds, their clothes, and their toys. They darted from room to room, exclaiming with joy over their new belongings. I selected matching outfits for them, and they were physically transformed from ragged orphans to cherished twins. They belonged, and they were clothed accordingly.

We spent the next few hours playing with the boys, setting up their room and also introducing them to the concept of a bathroom. They were accustomed to using bowls instead of toilets in their potty-training at the orphanage. I wasn't too confident in their ability to understand this unfamiliar system, so I played it safe with cloth diapers and lined rubber pants. That was new to them too. They'd lived their toddler years pantless and fancy free.

Orphanage life had been mostly discipline-free as well. *Pa fe sa* (Don't do that) and *Pa touche* (Don't touch) became two well-worn phrases in a matter of minutes. Chasing and monitoring our little Taz had us both mopping our brows. We were awed afresh at the stamina and stubbornness of our child and were wilting rapidly when we were pleasantly surprised by the arrival of the orphanage director, Joseph. He pulled up to our gate and honked the horn of a plush Toyota 4Runner. The boys, convinced that all horns honked especially for them, flew to the door, responding with their best horn imitations. "Keeep, keeeeeep!"

Jamison opened the gate, and we greeted Joseph, the Haitian man responsible for making TIH adoptions happen. According to Mark Riley, Joseph had been delivered by God from a life of drugs, alcohol, and immorality and now had a tender heart, eager to help the children of his country. Mark and his wife, Beth, had a deep love for Joseph, and had even given their blessing to the engagement of their daughter to him. The two had later broken off their engagement, but Joseph would always be a son and spiritual protégé to the Rileys.

As we shook hands with him, we tried to reconcile our background knowledge of Joseph with the large, stylishly dressed man in front of us. His polished shoes, ironed slacks, and button-up linen shirt accented with gold jewelry and shades made our conservative, not to mention soggy, missionary attire feel extra shabby.

Joseph offered to take us to a street-side restaurant—his brother's, he said—and a local grocery store. Thrilled at the thought of refreshment, we accepted. Soon we were seated in wobbly plastic chairs at *Bo Repo*, drooling at the smell of chicken on the grill. We drooled and smelled for forty-five minutes, shooing flies away from our Coke bottles and assuring our boys that we would get our food soon. In the meantime, we attempted conversation with Joseph—not an easy task. Thanks to the generator powering the restaurant, the stereo blasted *konpa* music to its patrons as well as the entire neighborhood.

Mindless of the noise, Joseph introduced us to his brother, who had just driven up—a police officer who, out of uniform, looked more like a gangster. He sat down at Joseph's table and ordered a beer.

With exhaustion setting in, boys on the verge of a breakdown, and konpa music rattling my brain, I began to regret our excursion. But a few seconds after the chicken and plantains were set before us, all was forgiven and forgotten. I'd never tasted anything so delicious.

"You say your brother is the restaurant owner?" said Jarod, surfacing from his feast and nodding toward the police-gangster, who wasn't as fluent in English as Joseph.

Joseph blinked for a moment, then nodded.

"Give him my compliments."

Joseph mumbled a few sentences to the policeman, and they shared a quiet chuckle.

"*Mèsi.*"

Finally satisfied, we wiped greasy fingers and mouths, then asked Joseph if we could stop for a few groceries.

"No problem," he assured us. And I soon found myself in a hole-in-the-wall mini market. There were few fresh foods, but lots of canned and packaged goods, imported from goodness-knows-where, with labels in Arabic, Spanish, and French. I grabbed a few things, hoping I'd be able to figure out how to cook in this land.

As we drove home from the market, the neighborhood grew gray, and makeshift kerosene lamps emerged in the booths of vendors trying to make a few last sales for the day. Joseph dropped us off at our house, and we began a routine that felt complicated but would soon become second nature: start the generator to power lights and fans, bathe the boys in cold water, brush everyone's teeth with bottled water, turn the generator off, and flip all the appropriate switches enabling our house to receive city power, should it happen to be given. Our bedtime prayers with our new sons were short, due to everyone's exhaustion, but straight from the heart. I blinked away a few tears as Jarod hugged Justin and Jaden close and bowed his head. "Father, thank you for bringing us safely here, and thank you for our sons."

Careful *not* to tuck our boys under the stifling heat of a blanket or even a sheet, we kissed them goodnight.

"I can't believe we're really here." I sat in our bed a few minutes later, helping Jarod arrange the mosquito net. "It's surreal." Once we were under the net, I collapsed onto my pillow. "I am so tired. I don't know how I'm going to keep up with those boys."

Jarod, too weary to converse, reached for my hand, then let it go when our hands instantly began to sweat.

"Hon," I murmured, "what do you think of Joseph?"

"I really don't know," was all he could manage.

I closed my eyes and drifted off, blissfully unaware of an oft-spoken Creole proverb that would define the years ahead: *Dèyè monn gen monn*—Beyond the mountains, more mountains. Had I known the shadows of those mountain paths—the toll the steep hikes would take on our family, my faith, and my health— my courage surely would have failed me. But by the grace of God, the God who can move mountains, I didn't know, and I slept in peace. In a pool of sweat. But in peace nonetheless.

# 2

# How Did We Get Here?

The Lord will fulfill His purpose for me.

Psalm 138:8

CHICAGO 2000

Jarod and I had been lounging on our hand-me-down couch, content in our newlywed life, when I bolted straight up and looked at Jarod like I'd never seen him before.

"Wait, what did you just say?"

For the split second my question hung in the air, I heard the typical men's dorm noises all around us—some version of hallway football that no mother would have allowed in her home—while the Moody Bible Institute students took a study break.

"I'd like to adopt," Jarod said again, still leaning against the afghan with our names and wedding date embroidered in a heart. "I've always wanted to adopt."

"*Always?*" I racked my brain for a memory of any past reference to said life-changing subject. *Mission field? Check. Papua New Guinea? Definitely. A love for kids? Yep. Adoption? Nothing.* "Uhhh, I don't think so, Hon. That definitely would have stood out to me!"

He shrugged, an understated response that would characterize our conversations for years to come. "Sorry. I thought I had."

The third-floor football game rocked the crystal candle holders on my be-doilyed coffee table, while visions of my future stampeded my brain.

"Are you gonna need to do something about that?" I waved toward the bedlam above us, but my resident director husband didn't seem too concerned.

I perched myself on the arm of the couch. "You do realize you kinda never mentioned this adoption idea in the whole three years we were dating, nor in the entire year we've been married?" I hoped he saw the twinkle alongside the shock in my eyes. But still . . . *seriously, Jarod?* "What if I hated the idea?"

"Well, do you hate it?"

I just squinted at him. "Tell me more. How did this start?"

"I guess with Dr. Badgero. So maybe that's not quite always," Jarod conceded.

"Ah." This was the missions professor everyone raved about. He'd left his position as the department chair the year I came in. "Okay . . . keep going."

"He and his wife adopted from a few continents. You knew that, right?"

I nodded.

"It was a calling to them, not just a last resort. Why not parent some of the millions of kids already out there? It's a mission field. An unreached people group."

I leaned my elbows onto my knees, letting these thoughts lead mine in a hundred directions. The football game upstairs had dispersed, but the stillness of the dorm was overtaken by the wail of a fire engine. Chicago streets were never silent.

"So you agree with him?" I finally asked. "You think adoption should be viewed as a mission? A calling?" But his answer was already clear. Part of me wanted to fight this wild idea. It could change everything. But the deeper I reached inside for my true feelings, the less I wanted to protest. I may not have sat under Dr. Badgero's teaching, but it seemed he'd turn out to have a lifelong influence on me anyway.

At that time in my life, I couldn't even have pointed to Haiti on a map. The facts of geography tend to exit my brain soon after they've entered. Jarod, on the other hand, has a long-term memory that files the maps neatly alongside everything else—kind of like study Bibles complete with concordances and atlases. But the tiny country of Haiti, which my brilliant husband informed me was just past Cuba, sharing island space with the Dominican Republic, was suddenly getting a lot of attention from us. This was the country with minimal processing fees, short waiting periods, and no adoptive age restrictions. The perfect solution to all the worst adoption hang-ups. Or so we believed. We opened our hearts to a child from that land of poverty and voodoo, more specifically from a little orphanage called "Truth in Haiti," started by Mark and Beth Riley.

I plunged into the sea of paperwork, cutting costs by compiling the dossier myself. I called government offices, filled out forms, researched social workers, and traversed the gray winter streets of Chicago to get papers translated, notarized, authenticated, and legalized. Then came the day of declaration. "How many children are you requesting?" I looked at the form. The answer was supposed to be simple.

*One. Right, Lord?* Again on my couch, framed by windows with a parking lot view, I surveyed our tiny apartment. Kitchen. Living room. Bedroom. Besides the obvious lack of space, our funds too were limited. Yet I wasn't ready to write my answer. There was that tug. A nudge. And my mom's question: "Don't you think it would be so much better to adopt siblings? They could face the challenges of adoption together. . . ."

I jumped off the couch, headed to the computer, and typed in TruthinHaiti.org. My fingers were well acquainted with the web address. I scrolled down the page of brown faces. Sometimes there were new kids, sometimes kids were taken off the list. *Were the twins still there? Or had they been chosen already?*

"Aha!" I clicked on their photo, searching the eyes of these tiny survivors, imagining. Imagining what Richard and Richardo had already lived through. Imagining them in my world.

*What am I thinking?* I shook myself from my dream. *How could this ever work?*

We were already asking Moody's physical plant if we could

knock out our living room wall to include an extra storage room in our apartment. That would suffice—*if* it was approved—for one child. But in order to have our home officially approved by the state for two children, we'd need twice that space.

But I wondered what else might be behind the wall. Ordinarily, I didn't venture into the men's space on our dorm floor; I was able to exit our apartment, take two steps to the stairs, and leave the building without any awkward encounters. But everyone was in class at this time of day, so I decided to risk some exploration.

Letting my door swing shut behind me, I turned the corner, opened a few closet doors, and landed on treasure: two storage rooms separated by a single bathroom. It was perfect. Absolutely ideal. *You see this, right Jesus?* I couldn't wait to show Jarod.

The second he was home, I launched my remodeling campaign. I had to show him the rooms before I could ask for twins. "It's perfect, isn't it?"

He was cautious, as always. But I pressed on. "Well . . . *if* we had that extra space. . . ." I tried to act casual, as if I hadn't already made up my mind. "We could consider siblings. They would always have each other." I felt my face flush as I tried to hold back the intensity building inside me. *How did I get so passionate about this so fast?*

Jarod nodded. He'd read all the same books I'd read. He knew the challenges adopted kids would face.

Thankful for even that degree of openness, I took it further. "Remember those twin boys we saw on TIH's website?"

I led him by the hand to the desk where the boys' picture was up and ready. "Just look at them. . . ."

41

*Are these our sons, God?* My hopes were rising by the second. But I couldn't let them lift off completely.

Jarod spoke practicality into the air, even as he squeezed me tight. "I'll admit it's a great idea. But we'd better wait to see what phys. plant says."

I wouldn't stop praying till we had our answer.

Jarod spoke with his boss the next afternoon, and she promised to present the idea to phys. plant. A couple days later, Jarod walked through our door, unusually sober. "Well, we've got our answer."

My eyebrows shot up while my heart fell. This wasn't the tone of victory.

But then I saw the corner of his mouth curl up as he made his announcement. "The idea has been approved. Moody will not only pay for the remodeling work, but physical plant will do the entire job for us."

I squealed my joy and threw my arms around his neck. "Can we do it? Can we adopt Richard and Richardo?"

"I'm all for it, if you are," he said, letting the smile escape completely. "But we are going to have to rename them. I think they'll thank us for it later."

We had Mark and Beth Riley on the phone in minutes, unable to relax until we'd claimed our sons. Several weeks later, I sent the dossier representing thousands of dollars and hours to Haiti, requesting permission to adopt not one but two of the nation's children. And thus our "three-to-six-month wait" began.

Our goal in waiting was to learn. How can we as a white couple best parent black children? How can we be prepared for the questions our children will ask later? What do we need to know about Haitian culture? We were facing a lot of new issues.

We discovered a Haitian Moody student's church plant. Soon attending his Haitian church in a Chicago suburb led to Creole language lessons. Before we knew it we were immersed in the culture of our children.

Inquisitive in our conversations with Mark and Beth as well, we learned startling truths about the condition of the church in Haiti. Mark's primary ministry was discipling a team of Haitian men, working with them to call pastors to repentance. According to the Rileys, pastors had some of the best-paying jobs in Haiti, due to their corruption, rumored to be third only to drug dealers and politicians. Instead of using their positions of power for the growth of Christ's body, their ambition was for their own little kingdoms. They preached vehemently against one another, grappling for the largest congregation and biggest offerings.

The key to a pastor's financial success was to form connections to foreigners, largely Americans. A pastor might stage a tour of an "orphanage" to receive monthly sponsorships for a nonexistent ministry, or simply invite a short-term missionary team to the worship service in his shell of a church building. Once he'd acquired generous donations for a "building fund," with little or no accountability from the well-meaning American donors, the pastor would throw a little money at the church and keep the rest for himself and his family. He'd grow fat, drive an SUV, and dress like the *gwo moun* (big man) he believed himself to be. His lifestyle served to underscore the heresy he preached: "faith" is the surest means to prosperity.

Mark and his ministry team prayed and worked for the transformation of these men, trusting that spiritual change within their congregations would follow. Once the true gospel was preached and lived out, Haiti might finally experience revival. In fact, Mark and Beth publicized their need for an on-field ministry administrator. "Hey, that sounds fun!" I joked, reading the update on their website. "We should do that!"

As the days went by, though, my lighthearted comment launched us into a more serious dialogue. The job in Haiti intrigued Jarod. I was shocked he would even give it a second glance, since he had been committed to Papua New Guinea ever since I'd met him. He'd always seemed so sure of his calling, and I didn't blame him.

The summer before his senior year in high school, Jarod went on a missions trip to Papua New Guinea, informing God it was only for the summer. His team's job was to lengthen and clear a runway in the thick of the jungle—in 130-degree heat alongside companions like eight-inch centipedes.

While the trip was designed by New Tribes Mission to challenge the young people, the most life-changing moment of Jarod's trip was completely unscripted—except of course by God. Jarod and several ten-year-old village boys braved the tropical sunshine, kicking a soccer ball with bare feet, wiping sweat from their eyes, when Jarod found himself surrounded by unfamiliar tribal men. Confused, he listened as the small men began a passionate speech in Tok Pidgin—the trade language of Papua New Guinea. Seeing his need for help, a missionary jogged to Jarod's side and translated into English.

They said they'd traveled the two days' journey over the mountain to find a missionary for their tribe. Their neighboring tribe, a completely different language group, had a missionary to translate God's Word for them, and now they were learning the way to heaven. These men, however, still did not have anyone to teach them the Bible, and their people were dying without God.

Jarod was gripped by their quest for truth. The mountain they'd walked from—dense with jungle foliage—loomed in the distance. But there was more.

The men, short enough to be dwarfed by Jarod's five-feet-nine-inch frame, were gesturing toward Jarod, announcing to the missionary, "We'll take this one. He can come with us and teach us God's Word."

As Jarod stood there, the missionary's Tok Pidgin words floating in the air, "*He can't possibly come . . .*," "*He's just a kid in his home country . . . must return to his parents . . .*," a fault line in his soul shifted. His dream of comfort was rocked, and his goal to follow his dad into a career of commercial piloting was shaken. In the span of a pickup soccer game, he'd received a call. The American Dream had crumbled.

A year later found Jarod in the concrete jungle of Chicago, a pre-aviation major at Moody, eager to someday fly missionaries to that remote Papua New Guinea tribe. When Moody began an Applied Linguistics program that same year, Jarod switched majors, now hopeful that he himself could be that tribe's Bible translator. Why would he not go serve in the land where he had heard his call to missions?

My call grew so quietly over the years that I sometimes doubted its existence. I'd grown up comparing the amber waves of Kansas grain to the harvest fields of souls in distant lands. Missions emphasis weeks and missionary biographies filled my heart with a passion to go and make disciples. Yet I prayed for writing in the sky or an audible voice to confirm it all. After all, it was music that had defined my high school years; I spent half my childhood at the keys of the brown grand piano in the living room. Shouldn't I use that gift? Major in piano? The road less traveled, the road to an unknown country, was just that—unknown. I didn't have a map to get there, and as much as I longed to be Amy Carmichael or Elisabeth Elliot, I knew my weakness for fashion, comfort, and self. Who was I to think I could follow in those kinds of footsteps? But still, Jim Elliot's words never stopped ringing in my mind: "Our young men are going into the professional fields because they don't 'feel called' to the mission field. We don't need a call; we need a kick in the pants."

The Holy Spirit, through the words of Jim and Elisabeth Elliot, "kicked" me into Moody's International Ministries major. I asked God to at least please show me the area of the world he wanted me in. When Jarod and I became acquainted through "brother/sister" floors during my sophomore year, I was both impressed with and jealous of his clear-cut future. *It would be really cool to see him twenty years down the road*, I thought. *I bet God's going to do some neat things through him.* He was a senior, ready to graduate and get on the mission field. He'd even told God that after three years of looking for the right girl to take along with him—to no avail—he was now putting girls out of his mind. But as God would have it, I would eventually mess up that part of the plan.

Jarod was the resident assistant of his floor and made it his goal to unite a diverse group of guys as well as reach out to us girls on their "sister floor." We enjoyed intramural sports, outings all over the Windy City, prayed and sang together, and shared each other's burdens. There would eventually be five marriages between the guys and gals on our bro/sis!

During the first semester of all our fun, Jarod somehow fell in love with me. I was oblivious to this turn of events and was busy setting him up with a friend on my floor. He wisely decided to clarify matters. He left a note on the bulletin board of my dorm lobby, baiting me with "top secret information" if I could find a few minutes to talk. This was nothing too unusual—he frequently left notes with silly poems or dramatic news for all of his "sisters." I laughed, showing it to my roommate Mary as we ran to class in the October sunshine—late as always. Once situated inside and recovering from our sprint, Mary whispered, "So are you going to say yes?"

I gasped. "Mary!" My stomach flip-flopped at her innuendo, but I let it go with a roll of my eyes. We would have continued to discuss it, but the professor was opening with prayer, of which I heard not a word. There was no way Jarod, practical "jungle boy" of all people, was going to get mushy on me.

But as Jarod and I took a quick walk to Walgreens during morning break, I was mystified. We small-talked all the way there and small-talked all the way back. Nothing too interesting, nothing too scandalous. In short, disappointing.

"So what's the top secret information?" I demanded, swinging my Walgreens bag as we crossed the last intersection before Houghton Hall.

His whole body grew rigid. "I'll tell you when we get inside!"

*Well, excuse me!* I didn't say it out loud, but the sassy look I gave him should have scared him all the way back to Ohio.

He opened the door for me and led me to one of the stiff and horrible dorm couches of Houghton's lounge. He sat across from me and started bouncing his legs.

I stared at him, waiting. *I don't think this could be any more awkward. What is his problem? Have I done something wrong? Is he about to confront me?*

And then he opened his mouth, and I just knew. *This is it. He really does like me. Oh man, seriously? This is where he's going to tell me? This is where "Moody Couples" cuddle! I'm going to die.*

And then, more importantly, *What am I going to say after he stops talking? I've only had ten seconds to think about this!*

Praying that some answer would come to me, I tried to listen. There was something about him hinting through his notes, his calls, his attention. Had I noticed? Was our friendship in jeopardy? How did I feel about him? Would I like to go out and talk more sometime soon?

My own inner turmoil eased a bit as I realized his must be even greater than mine. He couldn't seem to stop bouncing his legs. Soon the bouncing distracted me completely. I finally reached over and patted his knee. "It's okay, Jarod. I like you, you really don't have to be so nervous."

I stood up. "I'm free tomorrow night if you want to talk more."

Cheeks burning, I said goodbye and rode the elevator to the ninth floor. I burst through door 912, now shaking. "Mary! You'll never guess what just happened."

But she calmly repeated her previous question, "So, did you say yes?"

The following night, Jarod and I walked several blocks in the crisp fall darkness to Lou Malnati's pizza joint. Although our chocolate chip dessert pizza had my stomach swooning, when Jarod began speech number two in earnest, my attention quickly transferred to him. His legs may have been bouncing once again under the cover of our red and white checkered tablecloth, but he was speaking with a whole new level of confidence, and I met the gaze of his blue eyes with surprise and respect.

While I'd always been a romantic—appreciating charm as much as any female—I'd long ago decided I wouldn't give my heart to any man whose focus was shallow. As Jarod explained the depth of his interest in me, based on my character, my standards, my commitment to God, and finally my personality and looks, I knew he was worth listening to. I'd known all along he was a great guy, but I was soon pinching myself as this great guy said all of this to *me*. I sat, fingering my necklace, speechless except for a quiet "thank you," and he continued. He was asking me to be his girlfriend, he said, but even more importantly, he wanted me to know that he was pursuing me with the intent to marry. He had already been praying about us for a long time, and he wasn't just fooling around. Again, he said he realized I might not be ready with a response, but he was willing to wait for me.

Had he been asking me out to dinner that weekend, my yes would be been instantaneous. But hearing the *m*-word from his lips gave me reason to pause. I couldn't bear the thought of rushing in only to have to break his heart several weeks down the road. Grateful for the space he was giving me, I assured him I'd be praying over the extended weekend just ahead, and would give him an answer after.

He paid our bill, left the tip, and we were back out in the sparkling chill. I glowed the whole way to the dorm. *This guy really likes me,* I marveled. But I couldn't help but wonder: *Am I called to Papua New Guinea?*

I spent the long weekend with my aunt and uncle in Wisconsin, using most of my waking hours looking for an answer. Elisabeth Elliot, the friend and mentor who wasn't actually aware of my existence, offered words of wisdom in her book *Quest for Love.* And God met with me in the gray drizzle on the streets of Port Washington. He didn't really speak, but He listened as I plied Him with questions. I told Him all about Jarod's qualities and let Him know I'd sure appreciate some word on "this whole Papua New Guinea thing." The only answer in the mist was peace. A peace to go forward with Jarod. And faith to let God work out the rest of the details in His time.

Three years later, there we were, married, living in Dryer Hall, ready to adopt twins from Haiti, asking God about "the whole Papua New Guinea thing" all over again. The more we talked and prayed about Truth in Haiti's need for missionaries on the ground, the more we wondered.

We held hands on the white couch, trying to picture our future, Jarod describing the videos on voodoo he'd watched in his World Religious Systems class. He had seen footage of Haitian women wringing the necks of chickens in voodoo ceremonies and demon possessions causing animalistic behavior in the infamous mud pit. It had turned his stomach, he told me, and he'd thanked God he wasn't called to go there. Then again, he pointed out, he'd also told God not to get any ideas when he signed up for that "just for the summer" missions trip to Papua New Guinea, not to mention his declaration that he was "finished with girls" his senior year. How many times had God smiled in irony as Jarod told God how things would be?

We couldn't ignore the tugging in our hearts. We traveled to Haiti with Mark and Beth a few months later, and there, drenched in sweat, chasing wild toddlers, we answered the unmistakable call to serve in the very place Jarod had been determined to avoid.

# 3

# A Matter of Perspective

Give thanks in all circumstances.

1 Thessalonians 5:18

PORT-AU-PRINCE 2002

I had no clue how our parents would respond. Jarod and I were dropping a lot of bombs on them these days. A year and a half ago we'd blindsided them with our announcement of international adoption . . . of twins. Shortly after, we surprised them again with news of an unexpected mission field. Today, no more than two short weeks after our big move to Haiti, we introduced Daphne to them via cell phone. We were adding an eight-month-old daughter to our family. But though they sounded dazed, each parent congratulated us and graciously refrained from questioning our sanity.

The thing was, Daphne was irresistible. My heart was drawn to her the minute I laid eyes on her. I'd been in Haiti on a short trip prior to our move, and met Daphne at the ministry house, in the arms of Claire, an American visitor, who planned to adopt her. I'd wandered into the tiled living room to shoot the breeze (or rather complain about the lack of it) as Claire announced she was running Daphne back to the orphanage.

"I'll take her for you," I offered, eager for her to accept. "I was going to peek in on my boys soon anyway."

Claire thanked me and handed her over, much to my delight. Holding Justin and Jaden was a workout. Not because they were huge—they weren't. But they were wiry, bursting with energy, and oh-so *boy*. But this china doll was made of completely different stuff. Instantly smitten by her wide eyes and delicate features, I worked to win her heart. As I mustered all my charm to turn her sober stare into a smile, Pastor Mark passed by and commented on my efforts.

"Uh oh! You want a little girl too, don't you?"

"Ha! Well, maybe someday. . . ." But even as I downplayed the idea, I made a silent agreement with God that if for some unfathomable reason Claire was unable to adopt Daphne, I'd take that as His signal for us to claim her. Oh what a joy it would be to parent this dainty baby girl! But I had no idea how many others shared my sentiments.

A few months down the road, family circumstances prevented Claire from adopting, but by the time we got the news a Canadian family, the Walters, had already added Daphne to their list of adoptive children. But even with that announcement came the information that the Scheffer family from the States had their eye on her too. They told Pastor Mark they'd adopt Daphne if the

Walters changed their minds, and strangely enough, the Walters did. Little Daphne was "passed on" to yet another family.

Only days after our move to Haiti, Tadd Scheffer appeared at our gate. We'd become acquainted on a previous trip, so we were delighted to see him again. He greeted Jarod and me conventionally, that is, drenched in sweat, as he recovered from a walk in the heat with the help of *Limonade*, Haiti's glass-bottled limeade. In the wake of our pleasantries and the explanation of his visit, I offered him our congratulations.

"What for?" he asked, wiping his mouth and moving toward the shade.

"You're going to adopt Daphne now, right? We heard you were going to if the Walters didn't."

He took another swig, and I wished I had my own limeade. We hadn't splurged on bottled drinks yet. I made a mental note to do so soon.

"Actually," he said, chuckling, "that's a funny story. We did want to adopt Daphne, but things are getting crazy."

Jarod was distracted, saving Jaden from self-inflicted doom on a ledge in our cement yard, but Tadd instantly had my undivided attention.

"How so?"

"As soon as we chose to adopt Elijah and Annecy, Charity got pregnant." He kicked a rotting mango to the side of the yard. "That's gonna make for three kids in the same age range. Then when we said we'd take Daphne, we got pregnant again! We've decided five toddlers at once is more than we can handle." He laughed again. "So we're not going to adopt her.

I guess I'll just apply your congratulations to our baby, if that's all right."

"Of course!" I shot a wide-eyed look at Jarod. *God, did you really keep her available all this time for us?*

It seemed pretty obvious that He had. Jarod and I were tempted to bring her home from the orphanage that very day, but held ourselves back to iron out the details with Pastor Mark, not to mention pretend we were wise, responsible adults who would take more than five minutes to claim responsibility for a third child while still new to the country and parenting in general. But we'd jumped off so many cliffs recently, this one didn't intimidate us at all, like riding a roller coaster three time in a row numbs you a little to everything that scared you silly the first time around. In only a few short days, with some extra thought and prayer under our belts, we made yet another momentous walk over to the orphanage and came home a family of five.

Daphne's middle name simply had to be Joy. She was a ray of sunshine, lightening our testosterone-laden home. Music and giggles bubbled out of her even though she couldn't yet talk. When Jarod and I were in need of a little stress relief after the kids were tucked into bed at night, we'd snuggle our baby girl into our arms again, secretly thrilled when she woke up and entertained us with her silliness. Our family felt complete. Now all we needed to do was add Daphne to our paperwork and make the adoptions legal. And since we were living in-country, the process should be fast-tracked. *Maybe by Christmas? For sure by next year at this time!*

This new life as mom and missionary felt right in so many ways. I loved it and embraced it on one level—the level of all that truly mattered. On the shallow level, though, my speckled mirror reminded me my new callings were anything but glamorous. No matter how many cold showers I took, what kind of lofty promises my deodorant made, or how often I tried to get a little makeup to stick to my perspiring face, the fact remained: this Kansas wildflower had clearly been cut off from whatever was keeping her pretty (namely hair dryers, curling irons, and air conditioning). I was just going to feel wilted, droopy, and faded, probably forever. Why couldn't I be an orchid? The kind who looked even better in a tropical climate, one of those beauties from the movies that pulls off sweat and grunge with nothing worse than a cute dirt smudge on the cheek? And then there were the smells. The smells of *me* that I hadn't even known were possible.

The Cinderella-like task that best complemented my stepsister-like beauty was hand-washing cloth diapers. The pile accumulated each day, and its stench threatened to kill. The washing machine wasn't an option when city power was off, so I forced myself to soak, scrub, bleach, and rinse them by hand each night. I counted each diaper and announced the grand total to Jarod in self-gratifying triumph. My skin grew raw, and my attitude wasn't much better. I'd babysat a lot back in my Chicago days—I'd had a taste of parenthood in the States. But this? This was different. None of the parents playing Baby Mozart videos and buying memberships to the children's museum knew what this was like. They went through their disposable diapers without thought, started their washers and dryers with laughable ease. Of course, that hadn't bothered me back then, but today it did—now that I was "suffering." Yes, I wanted to be here; I wanted to be a mom on the mission field. *But could I whine for just a little while about how hard it was turning out to be?*

And at the same time, thousands of Haitian women bent their own weary backs over plastic basins of soapy water. Their hands weren't raw, because time had toughened their skin. Their hearts too had toughened when the fathers of their children didn't stay, didn't provide. They scrubbed cloth clean for a few gourdes, for the hope of feeding their children at the end of the day. And in the evenings as I stood outside my kitchen door and breathed in a few breaths of the same air those women breathed, I slowly remembered my joy; that true joy has nothing to do with circumstances, and is never found in comparison.

Life continued in a bizarre mix of heavy, sticky slowness and dizzying craziness. I battled messes, stretched my culinary creativity, and considered the day a success if any of God's grace had shown through despite my exasperation. Justin talked nonstop. Daphne wanted to be held. But Jaden was like no child I'd ever met. He was the very embodiment of hyperactivity. An attempt at ADHD meds sent to us from a doctor in the States changed nothing. Jaden had no interest in using toys for their prescribed functions. When his attempts to throw everything in sight were met with tough love, he settled for balancing things precariously on steps, chairs, or a table for the joy of the satisfying clatter sure to follow. The louder the crash the better. Any nonpercussive object was dragged; he trailed jump ropes, stuffed animals, or even T-shirts behind him, but soon grew weary of the quiet boredom and resorted to swinging them wildly against anything else that he could possibly knock over. *Why?* I didn't know if he could help it—was this just orphanage behavior, lack of discipline for the first few years of life?—or if this was a special need meriting compassion instead of discipline. *How hard do we push? What standards do we set?* Part of me wanted to shake him. But mostly I just wanted to show him how great life was when you pushed a toy car, or stacked the blocks, or put the puzzle together. I longed to climb into the mind of our perpetual-motion machine and turn everything down a notch. The poor boy couldn't even fall asleep lying still. He'd lie on his stomach, flopping his torso up and down in a steady rhythm until overtaken by sleep.

But it wasn't just hyperactivity. Jaden also had a temper, and an iron will, which tended to flare up at inopportune times. Restaurant visits, complete with Jaden's favorite food—rice and beans—often elicited a normal, delighted response. But if the cook dared take too long, his fury would build. To protest one such wait, he spewed each (adequately cooled) bite onto the ground. Our rebukes and warnings only fed his rage. For the good of our son and everyone else in the restaurant, Jarod escorted Jaden to our truck cab/sauna, where "detox" took about twenty minutes. Once back in the restaurant, Jaden devoured his rice. It wouldn't be the last time we'd wonder why he'd insist on making his own life miserable.

Then came the afternoon we realized Jaden's physical challenges too extended beyond what we'd surmised, the afternoon I walked past his room, finding his tiny frame convulsing on his bed.

"Jarod! Come here!"

He came running, Justin close behind. Daphne, already in my arms, clung to me, but I passed her to Jarod so I could tend to

Jaden. I sat down on the bed and pulled him onto my lap. *What is this, God? Spiritual or physical?* I prayed, but felt helpless as his arms and legs continued flailing, short cries bursting out every few seconds.

He finally stilled, rolled onto his stomach, pounded his head against his pillow a couple times, then yielded to sleep. We all exhaled, as drained from fear as Jaden was from exertion. But I wanted answers.

In seconds, I was across the street, demanding to know if the orphanage workers had ever witnessed a similar episode from the child who'd been declared "normal" and "healthy" by the visiting psychologist.

"*Wi*," they answered calmly upon my inquiry. "He does that sometimes. He has seizures."

I stared and sputtered. *Was this not important enough for anyone to mention to us? "Normal"? "Healthy"? This system is messed up.*

All we could do was talk to our doctor friend on the phone. Dr. Kim couldn't properly evaluate Jaden from the States, and therefore couldn't prescribe treatment, but told us to keep watch, and comforted us with the idea that children frequently outgrow seizures. "God hears"—the meaning of Jaden's name—was all we could count on. Without trusted pediatricians, therapists, or even any proper diagnosis in this confusing new country, we could only stumble our way one day at a time down the path that would someday, hopefully, lead us closer to an understanding of his special needs.

I knew our children's birth mothers were living. Mark and Beth Riley had told us as much. But somehow I'd let myself forget about them in those first few weeks. Justin, Jaden, and Daphne were *ours*. We couldn't leave Haiti with them, we had no papers to prove we were their parents, but we were all in. Worrying about Jaden's seizures was our job now. Filling Justin's inquisitive mind with knowledge and planting the seeds of Truth in his heart was our privilege. Nurturing the baby girl that God had providentially kept available for us was our responsibility. We were their parents now.

But then came the reminder that we hadn't been their first parents. That our beautiful family was born out of brokenness.

I was returning from a visit to the orphanage, eager to wash my hands and cool off in front of a fan. I wasn't startled to see a woman's tall, bony frame immobile outside our gate. People often knocked, to ask for something. But the purposeful gaze set above her high cheekbones told me this wasn't a casual visit. She shrunk back for a minute, trying to compose herself.

I greeted her, attempting to put her at ease.

She finally looked at me, tears in her eyes, shoulders trembling. "My name is Siliana. I am the mother of Richard and Richardo."

Time stood still. *How does a mother meet the other mother of her children? What does she say? What is she allowed to feel?* Thoughts refused to come. Just too many conflicting emotions. Fear. Jealousy. Anxiety. Compassion. Gratitude. Love. They all tumbled together, and I wasn't sure how they'd sort themselves out.

But in the absence of rational thought, the Holy Spirit took over. Responding to His nudge, I opened my arms and embraced her. Her shoulders were frail. And her internal struggle had to be a hundredfold more intense than mine.

"Come in, Siliana." I prayed I was doing the right thing. "Come see the boys."

The metal gate groaned and screeched as I opened it.

"Jarod?" He would know from my tone that something was going on. I opened the porch door and wondered what Siliana would think of our home. It was so bare. So empty and hard. But I suddenly felt ashamed of its richness, its tiled floors and real beds, its running water and three bedrooms.

Jarod stepped out from the bedroom, where the kids were watching a Bible song video on the laptop.

The kids. *Are they going to cling to her? Do they know her? Love her?*

"Jarod, this is Siliana. Justin and Jaden's birth mother."

His eyes grew large as he too processed what was happening. He held out his hand, then completed the Haitian greeting—a kiss next to each cheek.

And then Daphne, Justin, and Jaden swarmed around us.

Siliana's eyes, angled like Justin's, lit up with her greeting, "*Bonjou Richard! Bonjou Richardo! M-gen yon bagay pou ou.*" She pulled two packs of cheese puffs out of the plastic bag she'd clasped. Justin turned his gaze on Siliana and his connection to her was obvious. He hovered beside her plastic chair, munching his powdery treat, while Jaden twirled, returning occasionally to devour another puff.

Our conversation echoed in the empty living room. Siliana seemed eager for us to know her story: The boys' father didn't stay in the picture long enough to know the boys existed. With a lack of resources and dwindling milk supply, she'd left the eight-month-old boys at the TIH orphanage. Even as I tried to imagine how much of her story she had left unsaid, she informed us that she and her siblings had been raised in orphanages as well. Her own mother and father, both still living, resided in *Citè Soleil*, the infamous slum a few miles away, but found nongovernment organizations (NGOs) to be the most viable option to raise their family. Jarod and I blinked, each of us wondering where to lay the blame for such a scenario. Questions. There were always more questions. *Could Siliana's parents not find work? How hard had they tried to keep their children? How many of Haiti's orphans weren't actual orphans? How could the tangled mess of this country ever hope to be sorted out?*

Justin interrupted the second of silence. "*Mama!* Come see my bed." We followed as he pulled Siliana into his room. She sat on his mattress, expressing appropriate awe at his room, toys, clothes, and shoes. Almost all of it had been given to us—gifts from baby showers—and it was only enough to fill a Rubbermaid tub, but I still felt it was too much in front of her.

Jaden used his bed as a trampoline, and I remembered to ask Siliana about his seizures.

"*Wi!*" Her face grew sober, and she dove into the story of the boys' birth. I clung to each word, desperate to understand her story, but her speed and unfamiliar contractions left me scrambling. Thankfully, Jarod's nods and responses proved he was catching more than I was. I asked for a translation.

She'd nearly died during delivery. Justin was born without problems, but Jaden spent too long in the birth canal. By the time he came out, he'd turned completely black. The lack of oxygen prompted seizures and severe brain damage. Prescriptions that might have helped in any way went unfilled. Though Siliana knew her son had serious medical problems, there was no money for further doctor bills. She nursed and cared for the boys until they grew too hungry for her to manage.

I sighed, filled with emotion. "I'm so sorry." *How do I even begin to express the right thing to her?* I shook my head, and she seemed to understand.

"It was the grace of God we did not die. *Se gras Bondye.* . . ."

I nodded. "Almost two years ago. . . ."

"*No. Twazan,*" She said.

"Three years?"

"Yes they were born in 1998."

My eyebrows shot up. We'd been told 1999.

"How often do you visit the boys?" I asked.

"Every month. I always bring them *Chicos,*" she said, referring to the cheese puffs. She smiled. I was amused that Haitian kids loved the same junk food Americans kids were addicted to.

If she'd come every month for the past two years, no wonder Justin knew her. Jaden seemed to be taking her visit in stride, calling her "mama" just like any other female, but he didn't seem to have quite the same bond with her that Justin did.

When she finally stood to leave, we kissed her cheeks again, welcoming her to continue her visits in our home each month. It felt like the right thing to do, and I prayed it wouldn't backfire. Her eyes echoed her "*Mèsi,*" and she leaned down to kiss the boys goodbye.

She walked out of the gate and onto the gravel, and I held Justin, assuring him his "Mama Siliana" would be back another day. He sobbed uncontrollably. In spite of my attempts to comfort him, the pain of a broken world wedged its way a little deeper into his tender heart and mine. Adoption might be beautiful. But it's born out of anguish and mess.

# 4

## Diving In

As in water face reflects face,
so the heart of man reflects the man.

Proverbs 27:19

This was as close to boot camp as I ever wanted to get. I had no idea where I would find energy for the days—let alone years—ahead of me. Chores I'd barely noticed in the States suddenly consumed my life. The appliances and luxuries of life in the States were a distant dream to me now; if something was going to get done, it would be done by my own two hands. And my hands were tied up with kids. And they itched. The mangos I was falling in love with were producing a relentless rash—a wake-me-up-in-the-middle-of-the-night kind of itch—all over my fingers. All in all, life had become more work than I'd thought possible.

Mark and Beth had explained that I might want to hire house help. I'd dismissed that awkward idea at once. I was raised on a Kansas farm, for goodness' sake; we took pride in hard work.

Plus, I'd held housecleaning jobs in college—one involving nine Persian cats and conditions that made me fear for my health. I didn't want to send the impression to my new neighbors that mundane work was beneath me. But the longer I was there, the more I began to understand. Life required help. I was no longer part of an individualistic culture. Here help was gladly given and easily asked. Furthermore, Haitians jump at the chance to work a reasonable job for a fair wage.

My last and biggest hurdle, though, was the issue of privacy. Hiring a housekeeper meant another woman would watch me parent, see my possessions, and share control of my home. In theory, I'd never want to make that compromise, but fatigue and raw, itching hands trumped theories. Besides, hiring a helper would help my Creole vocabulary pass the three-year-old level and possibly provide a new ministry opportunity. So a tiny, smiling, thirty-something Madam George graced our home three days a week. It took me almost a year to learn her given name, since married Haitian women are always called by their husband's first names.

I'd imagined Madam George would plunge immediately into household chores. But her first priority, much to my confusion, was to rebraid Daphne's hair. I was as ignorant about ethnic hair care as I was about managing house help. So I watched and learned. My new (and unattainable) goal was for Haitians to never be appalled at my care of Daphne's hair again. I made a note to stay one step ahead of Madam George on that account. I'd much rather bond with my baby than mop the floor.

When I expressed my desire for help making meals, she offered to shop the open market and cook some Haitian staples. I was delighted. I put in my order for rice and beans and chicken and carefully counted the Haitian gourdes into her hand. About an hour later, she marched in out of the sun with her ingredients—most noticeably the chicken, alive and squawking. I hadn't even considered the dead-versus-alive meat option. I'd helped my mom butcher chickens one long-ago educational summer and had no desire to refresh myself on that process. But hey, if Madam George wanted to go to all that work, so be it. *Then again*, I thought as the hours ticked by and we all grew hungrier and whinier, *there has to be a faster way.*

Next market day, I carefully ordered chicken legs *only*. "Do they sell the legs separately?" I asked, to be sure.

"Oh yes, yes," she nodded, a little deflated by my lack of zeal for the entire bird.

"The other chicken was wonderful," I reassured her, "but it was too . . . expensive."

That she could understand. We'd had quite a feast the other day by Haitian standards, even though the chicken was tiny.

Upon her return from the market, I followed her to the kitchen to inspect this tamer form of meat. She unwrapped her purchase, and I froze, mentally replaying my instructions to her about chicken legs. *Pye poul, right?* But no. *Pye* would get me exactly what I saw before me: a dozen bony chicken *feet*, claws and all. What I'd really wanted was *cuisse*. Thankfully, Madam George had the presence of mind to buy a couple chicken thighs too, just in case the feet—a Haitian favorite—weren't enough for us hungry Americans.

I knew I had to learn to manage the open market myself eventually. So one morning I announced to Madam George that I'd be going with her. I placed the boys in Jarod's care and arranged Daphne in my handy baby backpack. Madam George stared at me and the contraption on my back, searching for words.

"The open market is no place for babies," she finally managed to say.

"Oh, she'll be fine," I insisted. "She likes riding in here." I bounced out of our yard and started down the hill, proud of my adventurous spirit. Poor Madam George trailed market bags behind me, helpless in the wake of rubberneckers. Apparently tall white women with Haitian babies on their backs were rare in those parts.

We arrived at the market, where makeshift plank tables crowded under tarps and rag "roofs." Carrots, papayas, oranges, and parsley piles lined the tables, fifty-pound bags of rice, beans, sugar, and flour sitting on the ground beside them. The air was heavy with garlic, onions, meat, and sweat. I wished I could filter out the less desirable aromas. Flies and conversations buzzed everywhere. Some women bargained calmly, while others barked out their demands. I longed to absorb everything in obscurity, but the environment changed as people took notice of us.

Within minutes, fingers wagged and eyes sparked. *What was that crazy white woman doing with a baby at the market?*

"*Blan*, she needs a hat!"

"You should be carrying an umbrella, *Blan*!"

I didn't know enough Creole to understand much more than the not-so-endearing term for "foreigner," but as the women crowded around me, grabbing at Daphne to "rescue" her, I understood I'd made a big mistake. Daphne began to cry, then scream, and I longed for words to voice my indignation. Wrestling her back into my possession, I fought to stay calm. *As if anyone thinks twice about taking a baby to buy groceries in the States. Really, people, no one thinks I'm stupid back there!* But, of course, I wasn't in Kansas (or Chicago) anymore. My petite friend did her best to hide her wry smiles, disperse the crowd, and buy our necessities. But I read her thoughts loud and clear: *I told you so!*

Once Jarod and I became slightly more familiar with the job of parenting, we also sought to develop relationships with the TIH team. Abraham, David, Stevenson, Evens, Jean-Paul, Simon, Jackson, and Joseph were an interesting assortment of men. Some were married with families, and some were single with stylish clothes and lots of cologne.

Pastor Mark believed them to be the "dream team" for the revival of Haiti, and reveled in their stories of spiritual warfare, moved by their impassioned prayers and emotive worship. Mark himself was a keyboard player and worship leader who had translated and recorded hundreds of songs into Creole. He'd formed the group into a band, and they frequently sang and played together at their own meetings, in the open air, and in numerous churches. He'd spent the past few years discipling this team in the subjects of revival, prayer, and worship, taking fatherly pride in the team members who could recite his lessons and sermons word for word, matching even the very inflections and emotions he had preached with.

Since Mark was only in Haiti sporadically, it was up to Jarod to oversee daily prayer meetings at the ministry house, a short walk up the rocky hill from the orphanage. It wasn't long, though, before Jarod saw major discrepancies in passion levels depending on Mark's presence or absence.

Jarod came back one morning around ten as usual, sweat-soaked and frustrated, ready to share a description of the TIH "worship" service he'd just attended. The few who had actually come were late. They'd murmured a few praise songs, then bowed for prayer. But after a few minutes of silence, Jarod realized they'd bowed themselves into sleepy oblivion.

Sure, a majority of the earth's population would consider praying for the revival of Haiti tedious. But these guys were supposed to be the "dream team." Surely an hour of prayer each day would be too little for these fervent men. We considered the possibility that we were making cultural blunders, but the fact remained that the men themselves led the worship sessions—a task they were quite capable of performing in front of any crowd.

We gave the matter time and prayer. Nonetheless Jarod came home with the same report each day. Day by day, their zeal dwindled, the meetings grew shorter, and the men's free time increased. Rather than pursue ministry, the men sat under shade trees around checkers boards, commenting on the women passing by.

Once Jarod was certain the issue needed to be addressed, he consulted Mark on the phone. But Mark brushed Jarod's concerns aside, assuring him that something must be lost in interpretation. Jarod was new to the language and culture—it would be easy to imagine these things. Mark had been their spiritual father for years. He was sure everything was fine.

We began inviting their families over for dinner. Surely trust and friendship was best built over a meal. I cooked shrimp and angel-hair pasta with Tabasco sauce, served atop our plywood table. After dinner, I talked with David's young wife on our new hand-built couch, thankful for a chance to get to know her better. I'd already shared a few hours with her on an early visit to Haiti. It was unforgettable, watching this woman who'd longed for a baby suffer a miscarriage. She'd paced the floor of the ministry house bedroom, crying out to God in her pain, weeping for mercy, pleading for a miracle. Tonight, mixing her English and my Creole, I wanted to feel her heart and offer any encouragement or comfort I could.

But at the other end of my sympathy and sorrow for her loss, I was met with a hard, strange strength. Her face was set as she assured me she was fine. "I have faith, sister. I have learned God doesn't want me to suffer."

Wanting to understand, I repeated her statement as a question: "God doesn't want us to suffer?"

"No. If we have enough faith, we don't need to experience pain. He's our Father. He wants us to be happy." She spoke as if to teach me.

I blinked, dumbfounded. *What happened to "In this world you will have trouble?" or "I delight in insults, in trouble, in persecution"? Did the apostle Paul not have enough faith?*

"In heaven, someday, we'll be free of trouble, that's true," I offered, "but you know even the apostle Paul was told by God that the thorn in his flesh wasn't going to be taken away. He might not have been 'happy,' but he did have *joy*." I prayed my "Crenglish" was making some sense.

Her eyes told me she understood, but she shook her head in disagreement, and the conversation was closed.

I wondered, if Haiti had been my only home, if gnawing hunger, a bed of rags, and endless disappointments had been my only experience, would I be so willing to accept suffering as part of God's will? And even with my past full of blessings, there was no way I could know my future here in this unfamiliar land . . . or anywhere. Would I always believe His grace was sufficient? No matter what happened? I sat, half-listening to the chatter of the men and children around us in our curved living room. But even as I imagined how hard life must have been for Madam David, for every young woman or man of Haiti, God's Spirit whispered that Scripture was for all peoples. That the all-sufficient grace was promised to a man who knew hunger, shipwrecks, prison cells, beatings, and loneliness. No, grace always had and always would reach those who needed it most.

As we said goodbye, I mourned false faith, the faith that had become a work to merit God's favor. It was the religion of Haiti, taught almost everywhere, preached from "Church of the Redeemer" on the corner every Sunday. We'd attended there last Sunday, listening for Truth, for encouragement, only to hear, "Look at the missionaries and their faith. God blesses them with cars, houses, and money. Have faith, friends, and you too will have all of these."

Oh, the "faith" it would take to change this country.

While we lived in Chicago, all we could do was take Mark and Beth's word that Joseph was doing his all on the adoption front. But now that we were finally in a position to see for ourselves, Jarod wanted to become more aware of the entire process, especially Joseph's efforts. Joseph's explanation for the yearlong delay in our—and others'—adoptions revolved around Madam Francois, head of Haitian Social Services, also known as IBESR. According to Joseph, she refused to sign TIH dossiers, particularly for adoptive parents under the age of thirty. Whether she was on a power trip, out to make money through bribes, or simply did not care no one was sure, but TIH could not get dossiers out of her office.

Supposedly, Joseph was doing everything possible to understand and meet Madam Francois's demands, but what Jarod saw was not encouraging. Joseph was frequently found to be sleeping instead of attending scheduled appointments, and he had very little to show for all his "work." Jarod's concern led him to ask Mark for permission to be actively involved. In light of mounting pressure from other adoptive parents, Mark was ready to grant Jarod's request. The mission was losing money daily, as parents who'd been paying childcare fees began dropping support checks.

Jarod began picking Joseph up each morning to make sure he kept all his appointments. And as they visited lawyers, birth parents, and government offices together, Jarod absorbed a wealth of information—including valuable language acquisition from Joseph's Creole phone conversations, which he assumed Jarod could not understand. There were no answers yet—only more questions—but Jarod determined to keep his eyes and ears open.

Mark came down to Haiti again, and everything morphed back into shape. Even as we voiced frustrations and puzzlement at the attitudes of the ministry team, we witnessed renewed passion and spiritual fervor. Sure, everyone loved having Pastor Mark around; not only was he charismatic in personality, but he was also willing to be vulnerable. It was only natural that his presence would invigorate everyone. But still, why was there such a complete void of dedication in his absence? All we could do was scratch our heads and wait to see what happened next.

In light of the paperwork delays in IBESR and the regular adoption complications, Pastor Mark made a decision to involve the entire ministry team in the adoption efforts. Optimistic that progress could soon be made with increased forces, he called a team meeting to discuss each member's new responsibilities. And then Joseph entered the room with an armload of dossiers.

"You see these?" Everyone's eyes were on him. "These are the dossiers our lawyer was paid to do. Why do I have them? Because he left Haiti—without completing any of them."

Jarod and Mark were horrified. This wasn't just a delay. This was thousands of dollars down the drain. Hiring a new lawyer meant paying new fees. And there wasn't a single adoptive parent in the mood for news like that.

Mark returned to the States, and Jarod continued mobilizing Joseph and the ministry team. The process that had been described to us as mysterious and impossible began to make more sense. Yes, there were hundreds of places where adoptions could be held up due to incomplete or inaccurate paperwork, a change in law, or even corruption, but there was a logical process to follow, and Jarod realized that a meticulous, honest administrator could avoid a lot of setbacks.

Fred, the head of the Port-au-Prince division of U.S. Immigration and Naturalization Services (INS), reinforced this understanding and shed new light on Joseph's true character. As Jarod sat alone in Fred's office, his spirits sank, along with any hopes of Joseph's integrity.

"I've warned Joseph about this," Fred said, pushing his glasses back up his nose. "Submitting documents like this results in imprisonment."

Jarod stared at him, mind racing. No wonder Joseph had insisted Jarod make this appointment by himself. He'd known the papers in this dossier were bad.

Fred continued. "I know you didn't do this. This is classic Joseph. But let me show you the differences between original and falsified birth certificates. You don't want to be in the position of signing these papers off to the U.S. Government."

They spent the next fifteen minutes going over the paperwork criteria that would keep Jarod out of jail.

"Did you hear Joseph's news?" Mark asked Jarod on the phone. "Madam Francois has made her demands known."

"And?"

"She says there's a new fee for those under age thirty: three-thousand dollars per child."

Silence.

Mark continued. "I'll let the adoptive parents know. No one is going to be happy about the extra fee, but I can't help but thank God that Madam Francois finally made a clear stipulation."

We were conflicted. Was Joseph telling the truth? Did we have any choice but to trust him? Others paid the fees, which went directly to Joseph—the only TIH contact Madam Francois would allow in her office—and no receipts were issued. "This is a very sensitive situation," Joseph explained. "Madam Francois wants to help us even though she's a very difficult person. I won't be able to insist on a receipt." We waited and prayed, and eventually saw a few dossiers come out.

When we received unexpected funds, from Jarod's grandmother who had recently passed away, we marveled at the amount. It was just enough to pay the fees for our three children. *It must be of God*, we said, and so, despite our fears, we paid.

# 5

## Not Like the Brochure

Whoever digs a pit will fall into it.

Proverbs 26:27

I couldn't wait for my mom to meet her first three grandkids. They were as cute as three toddlers could possibly be, practicing "Gamma's" new name, bouncing seatbelt-free in our Blazer as we parked alongside the airport. I jumped out to greet Mom as she exited the building, shielding her from the baggage handlers and beggars. This was her first experience in a developing country, and even though I always viewed her as able to handle anything, I knew her first time in Haiti wouldn't be easy.

I could tell she was on sensory overload as she got acquainted with the kids inside the car. That was to be expected—I'd been on sensory overload with them since day one. But poor Mom was also privileged to drive through some of the worst of our fourth-world country at the same time. She didn't have much chance to process anything that first day. Once we pointed her to the room she'd share with Daphne, she started pulling treasures out of her bulging suitcases. It was Christmas in November. Within minutes, Daphne was in love with a new brown-skinned, almost-as-big-as-her baby doll, and Justin's voice was—of all things—*amplified* by a microphone attached to a childproof tape player. Jaden set to work balancing new cars and trucks on stairs, chairs, and tables, elated to have new clattering materials to work with. I was just happy to have my mom with me. Of course, the chocolate and cheese weren't bad either.

After taking in my new way of life over a few days—the heat, Jaden's issues, the stained scummy bathrooms, the poverty all around us—she finally broke down in tears at the kitchen table.

"I just don't know how you can do this." She used the collar of her T-shirt to wipe the beads of sweat off her upper lip, and she looked up at me, eyes reflecting what I'd already felt. "I mean I do," she continued. "I know God is helping you, but it's just so hard for me to imagine you staying here forever. . . ." She waved her hand at my kitchen, at my house, at all of Haiti.

The lighting was dismal despite a blazing sun on the other side of the cement-block walls, the indoor temperature had to be in the nineties, and the humidity equal to a sauna. The kitchen, in which we sat, was functional, but from an American perspective, a comical mess: no upper cabinets, a cracked peach flowered tile countertop, and two crooked rodent-friendly cupboards below. The two "windows" were formed by cement blocks specially cast with open designs allowing for breezes, which rarely came. Screens were stapled to a rough wooden frame and nailed against the inside of the windows to keep bugs out. But the bugs had missed the memo and poured through the gaps between the frame and the wall.

"Are you okay here?" she asked, really wanting to know.

*Was I?* I looked away for a second. It was hard here, I couldn't deny. A big part of me wanted to indulge in the sympathy she was offering. Yeah, I would totally prefer air-conditioning, shopping malls, and the Cheesecake Factory. But the other part of me knew this was exactly where I was supposed to be. Me: lover of style, comfort, makeup, and home decor. It was time for me to die to self. It hurt, the dying. But I did believe the other side of that death held the abundant life my soul craved. And I wanted that more than the alternatives.

I looked back into Mom's blue eyes. "Yeah. I really am."

And as she said goodbye, after two weeks of falling in love with her little brown grandchildren, celebrating Daphne's first birthday, and working alongside me, she knew I was in the right place, and allowed me to follow God's call with a grace and abandon few parents are able to manage.

Just a month after our boys celebrated their fourth birthdays, Christmas was upon us. It was my first year without a tree, without a sweater, no family gatherings, and no presents. (After all, my mom had spoiled the kids rotten only a few weeks earlier.) I steeled myself against the nostalgia that so often fills the holiday season. No, there would be no "Candlelight Carols"—the Moody music program's elegant winter tradition. No Christmas Eve with brothers, grandparents, uncles, cousins. No kids forced to re-perform their Christmas songs and poems before opening glittery gifts. It was just us. Just noise and heat and work. But Steven Curtis Chapman sang through our laptop speakers about how Christmas is all in the heart, how our God is with us, how Emmanuel did this very thing—left his home to reach us. My "incarnation" was nothing compared to His. Nothing.

I taught the kids "Away in a Manger," blinking happy tears as Daphne hummed and Justin pushed the words through accented lips. We told the story of Jesus's birth, setting up the olive wood nativity scene I'd bought a lifetime ago in Bethlehem. And we experienced the joy of sharing the story of Jesus's birth with our own children for the first time. It was sweet, and also as ridiculous and out of control as real life with three preschoolers can be. There was no magazine version of Christmas in this house. Just clear evidence in my own heart and those of my children that we were in desperate need of a Savior.

When Jarod's parents came to visit us in January, we experienced as much of an escape from reality as possible. They treated us to a two-night stay at Wahoo Bay—a European-style hotel a couple hours up the coast. Sadly, the air-conditioning didn't run twenty-four seven, and unfortunately there wasn't always hot water, but even so, we felt like we'd died and gone to heaven. We'd escaped the slummy life and were surrounded by beauty. Flowers and tropical foliage covered the grounds. Beach umbrellas and bamboo mats on wooden beach chairs dotted the sand, and we could fight the heat with either crystal ocean or pool water. I almost relaxed completely. Until, of course, I was interrupted by some near-death experience of a child. Or the dilemma of how to stop Daphne from devouring sand. Alas, my ideal vacation mode (eyes either closed or glued to a book) would simply have to wait another ten years. In the meantime, I settled for coconut milk fresh from the coconut— chopped open in front of me with a machete. And no meal prep. And no dishes. That was really as much as I could hope for.

Our last dinner at the beach, we splurged in the open-air restaurant. Jarod and I were tanned (one of my eternal ambitions), he sported a new shark-tooth necklace, and I was relishing a final meal during which I could depend on others to cook, serve, and clean up. It was glorious. But then I looked up at Jaden, sitting on Pa's lap across the table. My brain took a second to process what my eyes saw. *Did he really just bite into his drinking glass?*

"Jaden is chewing on glass!" I blurted out.

Everyone turned toward Jaden and gasped. Sure enough, his glass now sported a mouth-shaped hole.

"Jaden! Spit that out!" We all attacked him.

Jarod jumped up and grabbed the glass away. I shoved my fingers in his mouth to fish out the broken bits of glass, and Granny and Pa wiped up the spilled water. Justin shrieked and reprimanded his twin.

So it wasn't idyllic. But no one drowned, and no one's esophagus was punctured.

And then it was back to real-life issues. Jarod tackled the adoption monster with a ministry employee, Junior, at his right hand. I battled sweat, fatigue, cockroaches, termites, and laundry alongside Madam George.

Nothing could be simple. Doing laundry with my machine was only possible if we had electricity through *Electricite de Haiti*

(EDH), or through running our small generator. Tripping over my toddlers, I'd tote our laundry outside, down cement stairs, to the dark outside rooms where a curtain separated our guard Jamison's room from my washing machine. In the interest of conserving water, I'd catch my rinse water in a plastic tub and then scoop it back into the washer with a bucket to use as the wash water for my following load. My machine typically took half an hour to fill, thanks to poor water pressure, so I sought to remedy that problem by filling it with a hose. It sounded simple. But being easily distracted from the hose and plastic tub by child emergencies, I rarely escaped some form of water-related disaster. More days than not, I found myself frantically mopping the flooded floor with bath towels. Failure to do so would result in the destruction of Jamison's belongings. The constant process of wringing towels used for mopping quickly cooled my fervor to save water.

The laundry day to beat all others, however, was the day that Jamison's curtain partition blew to the side, revealing someone other than our guard lying on his bed. In that fraction of a second, I saw far more skin than I should have of a woman who was *not* his wife. The woman covered herself with a sheet, and I ran quietly back up the back stairs to consult Jarod. By the time he confronted Jamison, the woman, fully dressed, was being ushered out the gate by our now very worried guard.

"Who was that?" Jarod asked.

"She's a friend. She just needed a little rest. It was nothing."

We liked Jamison. He'd done a good job working for us. He was nice to our kids. We'd had his wife and two little sons over for a meal and had encouraged him to go home to them any time he needed to or even to have them over to his room any time. But as much as we'd appreciated him, we knew a naked woman in his room was no innocent mistake, no matter what cultural perspective we used. At the advice of both Pastor Mark and Wilber, the most trust-worthy member of the ministry team, we let him go. I hurt for his wife. And even though his choice wasn't our fault, I deeply regretted that his employment with us had separated him from his wife. Jarod and I vowed never again to place a guard in that kind of situation.

Wilber recommended a cousin of his as a replacement. And so Matye took Jamison's place.

Beth Riley flew in for a few days to lend Jarod a hand in the management of paperwork, and of Joseph. She'd loved Joseph like a son for years already, but couldn't deny that things didn't always add up when he was in the equation. She and Jarod decided to visit Junior. Maybe Joseph had confided in him. Junior seemed sincere in his desire to help the ministry—maybe he would open up to Beth and Jarod if he'd sensed anything fishy.

Junior and his wife greeted them outside their small cement home. Jarod and Beth were in a hurry, so they conversed outside.

"Joseph told you that the lawyer had taken our money and then left for Canada," Junior said, fanning himself with a rag.

"Exactly." Beth nodded for him to continue.

"Well, the truth is, the lawyer had been in Canada for an entire year by that time. He never took the money or the dossiers. The money was in Joseph's hands the whole time."

Beth and Jarod stared, jaws dropped.

"Now Joseph claims he passed the second set of fees and the dossiers on to our new lawyer, Met Avion, but you should talk to Met Avion to hear the truth about that." As Junior finished, his cell phone rang. He looked at the caller ID. "It's Joseph."

"Take the call," Jarod encouraged him. "I want to hear what he says."

Junior held the phone at an angle so everyone could hear. "Halo?"

Joseph's voice was tense. "I think Jarod is bringing Beth to your house to talk with you. Don't tell them anything. Beth will believe whatever you say. And don't worry about that little white guy. I'll take care of him."

Junior's wife too was listening with wide eyes, silently warning him not to tell Joseph what was going on. She was visibly shaken.

"Wi, wi," Junior responded and hung up. That was all the proof Beth and Jarod needed before driving to Met Avion's house.

Met Avion too was nervous. He wouldn't say much, but conceded that he'd never received funds or dossiers from TIH.

Joseph was caught. Two lawyers had been "paid," but neither had received the funds.

As Jarod mulled things over, more pieces of the puzzle clicked into place. References to "Joseph's restaurant," "Joseph's cars," and "Joseph's houses" had popped up frequently as Jarod rubbed shoulders with anyone who knew him. Joseph had been careful in Jarod's presence to refer to those things as "his brother's" or "his uncle's," but now the true reasons for the repeated "mistakes" people seemed to make as they referred to these things, not to mention Joseph's stylish clothes and gold jewelry, began to unfold. There was a lot of adoption money unaccounted for.

The news devastated Mark and Beth. Already adoptive parents were threatening lawsuits. Some had been in process a couple years—even longer than us. While a few families chose to trust God's sovereignty in the face of a tumultuous process, others were bent on justice or even revenge for the emotional turmoil they were suffering.

Mark and Beth weren't about to ask for another set of lawyer fees from these people. They'd rely instead on the ministry's general funding. To further ease the burden for adoptive parents, they made childcare payments optional.

While a few continued sending support for the care of their children in the orphanage, many others quit. Jarod and I couldn't fault them. We ourselves would have been drained completely dry had we supported our kids at those fees so extensively. But right or wrong, TIH now found itself in an impossible situation. Funds previously channeled to support the men of the ministry team were redirected to the orphanage. It was no small matter.

Each member of the ministry team was supported by TIH. Married men received additional support, and those with children received increases proportionate to family size. Mark and Beth longed to bless these men—their "spiritual protégés"—and their salaries weren't much according to American standards. But this system of support created total dependency. Though the money wasn't a lot in American eyes, their salaries still set them a level above their peers.

These issues might have come to nothing had the men of the team been as passionate about spiritual revival in Haiti as Mark believed them to be. He'd assured them he'd always do his best to bless their service with available funds, but also exhorted them not to count on a set salary. Of course when they received generous pay month after month, they believed themselves to be secure, making no effort to seek additional income. If they weren't busy with ministry duties (which was most of the time Mark wasn't in Haiti), they were content to play checkers on the roadside.

The announcement was made: salaries would drop drastically for a season. Pastor Mark promised to raise them again once the current state of emergency had passed. But in their panic, the men revolted. Cruel rumors surfaced. Threats and lies spread. And the Rileys, all too familiar with the bit of real estate between a rock and a hard place, wondered how things could possibly get worse.

Naturally, there was a way.

The Haydens, one of the more disgruntled adoptive families, had previously chosen a teenage boy from TIH, tragically diagnosed mid-process with HIV and declared unadoptable. Their heartbreak and his were unimaginable. They told him they'd continue to treat him as a son, even if he lived in Haiti—visiting, loving, and supporting him. At the same time, they chose another son—Jonason—whose age teetered dangerously close to the cutoff for adoption. Each day the process dragged on brought them closer and closer to his birthday, and each day the grief connected to the loss of their first son and anxiety for their second fueled their bitterness against TIH.

Jarod took immense care to make sure everything was accurate and in place before submitting Jonason's dossier to the American INS, especially in light of the warning he'd received from Fred. Jonason's birth certificate worried him; the copy in-hand was not an original and did not meet the criteria Fred had so specifically outlined. Determined to avoid setbacks, Jarod took Junior to locate the infant baptismal certificate, the most reliable document available.

They came back, successful after their three-day quest, bearing devastating news: The baptismal certificate—trumping all other documents—displayed his birth date an entire year earlier than anyone suspected. Jonason had been unadoptable the whole time.

We felt like we'd been sucker-punched. This news meant the end of TIH. It would surely result in a disastrous lawsuit. All that remained was to inform the Haydens. Jarod called Pastor Mark to tell him the bad news. But Jarod was completely unprepared for Mark's response.

"Jarod. . . . You've got to make that paper disappear."

# 6

## The Infertility Clause

If any of you lacks wisdom, let him ask God.

James 1:5

We needed help. As we cried to God for wisdom, our prayers jarred a memory of some friends who were currently living in Haiti. We'd not yet actually met them, but we instinctively knew they were trustworthy. Pierre and Yvette Cadet were Moody alumni, currently church-planting here in the country of their birth. We'd begun attending the Haitian church they'd helped plant in Evanston, Illinois, around the same time they'd moved their family back to Haiti. We knew of each other through our mutual friend who now pastored the Evanston church—Franz Lacombe, another Moody alum.

By the time we got their Haitian phone number and address, our dilemmas had compounded. The bottom line: Jarod would not compromise on falsified paperwork. The muddy middle line: We'd consider leaving TIH if they didn't change their stance. Entangled in both issues were our children's adoptions. They remained in the incapable hands of Joseph. Should we take a stand and leave, our adoptions could be doomed. But maybe, just maybe, the Cadets could shed some light on our situation.

Our drive up the mountains of Petionville to their home was not in vain. They welcomed us as if we were family, congratulating us on our beautiful kids, and offering to help us even before they knew how desperately we needed it. They had five young sons, a manic dog named Tiger, and countless chickens, making our lives with three kids suddenly feel oddly manageable.

When we explained our predicament to them, they didn't even hesitate.

"You need to get out of there."

My heart pounded at the thought. *No, no! We just joined TIH! Only a year ago we were singing their praises to all our supporting churches. We were so sure of our call. We'll look like fools. . . . Then again, maybe we are.*

"Do you think it's possible for us to find our dossier in IBESR?" Jarod asked. "Joseph insists they won't meet with anyone but him."

"Oh don't worry. We can get you in there." Yvette was so confident, we straightened in surprise.

Now here was some hope.

"Oh yes. We'll get you in there. It's all in how we present ourselves." As she launched into stories of how the right suits and attitudes landed her success in more than one Haitian government office, I was strangely reassured. If her main concern was a power suit and matching pumps, we might stand a chance.

It was settled. "We'll all go together, dressed in our best."

A few days later, the seven of us arrived, sweating in our finery, praying we'd be able to meet with either Madam Francois herself or Madam Clerveaux, who served directly under her. Jarod and I, our kids, and Pierre and Yvette piled out of the Cadets' SUV in the most orderly chaos we could manage, juggling kids, sippy cups, and diaper bags.

I looked up for a moment at the building before us. Only God knew how many children's lives had been affected by the choices made inside. The cement-block government offices weren't impressive—this was no national palace—but I wondered what kind of spiritual warfare took place unseen. This was about lives, about *souls*. The children of Haiti were deliberately kept in poverty by the corruption here. To the officials inside, it was about money, power, prestige. It was even about preventing "worthless orphans" from attaining better lives than them. This was the voodoo philosophy in action.

But *maybe* someone inside cared. Maybe. I prayed that someone would.

We signed in at a wooden desk, strangely situated on a porch. A young woman escorted us inside, and without explanation gestured for us to sit on a few wooden chairs in a bare hallway. She disappeared, and we waited.

It was normal to wait. Waiting constituted about 75 percent of the past year. But not all waits were this intense. Every toy thrown by Jaden, every outcry by Justin, every wiggle and giggle of

Daphne put me more on edge. *Oh please, Father, please. Let us get in. Let us find our papers.*

I looked the gang over one more time, now convinced that the wrinkles, dust, and juice dribbles would be our downfall. If I could just get them to behave . . . if we could just be perfect enough, maybe we'd stand a chance. I tortured myself with such thoughts for the first fifteen minutes, then resorted back to silent pleas. *Lord Jesus, you see us, I know you do. Let us find favor here. . . .*

As I began to return to a place of relative peace thirty minutes later, a brusque forty-something woman squeezed past us in the narrow hallway and opened the wooden door in front of us. Maybe Yvette's strategy of looking important would pay off, though at this point Pierre and Yvette were the only ones even close to looking sophisticated. My calm evaporated and my hands grew clammy.

The woman bid us *entre*, so we piled into the tiny office in as dignified a fashion as possible. She introduced herself as Madam Clerveaux, offered no smile and very little eye contact, and asked why we'd come.

As she seated herself at her desk, I almost let myself go. I was a breath away from kneeling before her, letting the tears roll, and producing the most gut-wrenching version of our adoption quest possible. I searched my mind for the right Creole words, heart pounding, wondering if my tongue could actually manage it. Would it work? I inhaled.

But it never came out. We'd brought Pierre and Yvette for good reason. Madam Clerveaux's empathy levels didn't seem too high anyway. I wondered if she could possibly be a mother.

The Cadets addressed Madam Clerveaux in French, signaling their high level of education, and I breathed a prayer of relief that I'd kept my mouth shut. I'd forgotten that French was a big deal to the Haitian upper crust.

I was quickly lost. The French was flowing, and the best thing I could do was hold kids down and pray. And I could imagine. I had enough faith to be able to picture a dramatic turnaround. God *could* do it. This woman could march our papers into the right office, secure the coveted signature, and we could be on our way. I knew my God could do that. *But would He?* He was proving so mysterious these days. His higher ways were pretty much unsearchable to me. I didn't get them. *But Lord, could you at least just help us find our dossiers?* That in itself was crucial. They were irreplaceable.

As the Cadets finished explaining our situation, Madam Clerveaux's face remained blank. I bribed continued silence from the kids with fruit snacks as she rummaged through her desk and file cabinets. Was she ignoring us or trying to help? At last she pulled a stack of papers out of a drawer.

She glanced them over and announced calmly, "Your dossier."

We all gasped. But not too loud—as if the papers would disappear if we weren't careful. She drew our attention to the yellow sticky-note on top of it, casually bearing what was to us, an anything-but-casual notation: Madame Clerveaux had informed Joseph eighteen months ago that Jarod and I were "underage" to adopt since we were under thirty-five. An exception to this guideline would be made only in the case of documented infertility.

Jarod stiffened in the chair beside me. "*Eighteen months ago?* Joseph has known about this for a year and a half?"

I looked at Yvette. "Infertility? We have to be tested? By whom? Where?"

Apparently Madam Clerveaux spoke a little English. "It must be in the U.S.," she said. "That is where your dossier is from. The test must be done there too."

I stared in disbelief. How were we supposed to have fertility tests done when we had three children who couldn't leave the country?

"Now if they are *not* infertile?" Yvette wanted complete clarification.

"Then they must wait until at least one of them is thirty-five years old," said Madam Clerveaux firmly.

She may as well have said fifty. An eight-year wait was unthinkable.

She handed Jarod our dossier and he thumbed through it. Adding insult to injury, Daphne's paperwork was missing entirely. He handed the papers back, and Madam Clerveaux instructed the Cadets that we should update it after we'd followed her instructions. With that we were dismissed.

"I'm guessing Joseph collected the funds and promptly 'forgot' about adding Daphne's papers to our file," he mumbled on our way out. "Funny, because he assured us she was included in Madam Francois's 'special favor.' We paid $3,000 for her nonexistent dossier to be released."

The truth sank in as we loaded our unraveling gang into the SUV and rattled our way toward home. Joseph had deliberately deceived us for the past eighteen months. He'd neglected to mention the "fertility clause," never submitted Daphne's paperwork, and worst of all, insisted our papers required a $9,000 ransom to be released from Madam Francois's office.

Our money was gone—straight into Joseph's pocket. And now we had to face the matter at hand: our only option was be tested or wait eight years.

We'd been married four years. We postponed having a family the first year, as I needed to finish college, but in the following three years had failed to conceive. I knew from even minimal research that couples were deemed infertile after one year of trying.

I held Daphne tight as we bumped our way up the hill to the house. "We may be in for a very ironic answer to our prayers."

"If we can even get the testing done," Jarod's said tersely. "We can't just leave our kids and fly back to the U.S."

"Yes you can," Yvette answered from the front seat. "We'll take them."

Somehow we knew that arguing with a woman like Yvette was pointless. All that was left to say was thank you.

By evening, we couldn't imagine feeling more drained. The fury and despair had coursed through us for a few hours, leaving us exhausted and empty. We'd come to Haiti on such noble missions—we would stir revival in a desperate land, we would rescue children, we would make a difference. But our hands were tied on every account. Feeling wooden, I cleaned up the remains of yet another rice-and-beans dinner while Jarod commenced the nightly feat of showering the kids. The chatter and squeals emanating from the bathroom rolled past my senses. All I knew was the fog that seemed to close in on us from all sides. The ministry "dream team" we'd come to lead was a disaster; Jonason's adoption crisis might force us out of the ministry; and now, thanks to Joseph's web of deceit, the best hope for our adoptions was infertility—documented by an inconvenient, unexpected, not to mention expensive trip to the United States.

Though my mind whirled in the storm of all these crises, infertility was the issue consuming me tonight. *How would it feel to have our adoption problems resolved in this way?* I couldn't possibly be truly happy to hear that we were unable to have our own children. The idea of blue-eyed-blondes (they had little chance of being anything else) carrying on some of our best and worst traits to future generations was as desirable to me as it was to anyone. To be declared infertile had the horrible ring of finality to it. But, on the other hand, we'd already been entrusted with the care of three precious souls. We'd prayed for these children since 2001 beside two empty white cribs in our Chicago apartment.

Then it hit me: We'd prayed beside two white cribs, not three. Daphne hadn't been a part of that plan.

"My ways are higher than your ways."

In reality, all the plans Jarod and I had laid together so far were spiraling out of control. But our ways were not God's ways.

Jarod finished the email as I read over his shoulder. He clicked send, and our question went out to the people we respected most. We wanted trustworthy mentors giving us wisdom concerning the line we knew we must draw. There was no way we'd sign before the U.S. government that everything in the dossier was, to the best of our knowledge, correct. The weight of that decision and its consequences felt like lead in our stomachs. We had no desire to feed "wolves," nor did we want to ruin the lives of the Haydens and their son. The cost was too great. It was a compromise we just couldn't make. But we wanted feedback. Was there anything we were missing? And did this mean we should leave TIH?

We also shared our developing thoughts on ministry in Haiti—how being raised with a voodoo worldview, even under the "Christian" label, had shaped the members of Truth in Haiti's team beyond recognition. The Spirit of God of course still had all power to transform lives, but if we were looking for a long-term strategy for spiritual change in Haiti, we needed to look at raising a new generation, whose worldview was still moldable. We longed to see the orphans of Haiti raised to think and live biblically. We shared a vision of raising orphans in Haiti, in family settings, with Christian house parents discipling them in the fashion God had always intended. We asked our mentors—some professors at Moody, some pastors and missionaries—if they had any knowledge of ministries already implementing programs of that nature. We hoped and prayed for helpful responses.

It didn't take more than a couple days to get replies. An email from Moody professor Dr. Steve Clark caught our attention immediately. He wrote of children's homes in the Dominican Republic, thriving under the direction of Kids Alive International. When Jarod and I investigated online, we were fascinated to discover the implementation of a vision very similar to ours in over a dozen countries around the world. We were further intrigued to discover that a Canadian family had just that year moved to Cap Haitian to open children's homes in Haiti. We clicked the "contact" link, requesting more information.

As God would have it, in a matter of days, we were able to meet Tom Froese, the Canadian, while he renewed a passport in the capital. Over the next few hours together, we found that the goals of Kids Alive matched our own too closely for us to ignore. By the time Tom left, a trip to Cap Haitian was on the agenda. While the proverbial door we had so passionately sprinted through only a year earlier began to creak shut behind us, we prayed that our trip to Cap Haitian might reveal an opening window.

Confirming what our hearts already told us, not a single mentor advised us to stay with Truth in Haiti. Everyone urged us to leave on good terms—to communicate love and respect, but to hand in our resignation nonetheless. We knew what we had to do, but that didn't make it any easier. We loved Mark and Beth, and we'd grown close enough to know that their hearts weren't set against the Lord or us. We knew this would hurt. On one level, we understood their perspective: They wanted to see Jonason adopted, and they knew how desperate the Haydens were to have their son. They were in a place of spiritual, emotional, and legal pressure that few people are asked to enter. We longed to preserve our relationship with our dear brother and sister in Christ, but our "black-and-white" versus their "gray" perspectives marked an end to our partnership. We prayed for courage to make the call and say the words.

# 7

# Our Disappearing Act

You who fear the LORD, trust in the LORD!
He is their help and their shield.

Psalm 115:11

The phone call was over and I knew my face and neck were a splotchy red, an annoying giveaway any time I'm worked up. At least Pastor Mark and the head of his board hadn't been able to *see* Jarod and me over the phone. As if that's what was important.

This had been *the* call. The call Jarod and I had dreaded; the call that felt completely surreal and a little too combative. Here we were, with one measly year of experience under our belts, standing up to our bosses with what had had to sound like holier-than-thou reasons for why we felt compelled to leave the mission. First of all, we announced that we could not in good conscience submit Jonason's dossier. Second, we let them know that we could no longer work alongside Joseph, whose lies about his restaurant, cars, homes, lawyers, and—most recently uncovered—the status of our adoptions and the misappropriation of our $9,000 were destroying everything. When Pastor Mark and the board director remained united in their decision to keep Joseph on board, our decision to resign became final. Their reasons were pragmatic: Should they dismiss Joseph, not only would they face possible retaliation from him, but they would also lose time and ground in many adoptions. They'd also need to find and license a new orphanage director—a process that could indeed be lengthy and complicated. Understanding this, Jarod agreed to help them wrap up loose ends for a few adoptive families before leaving.

I despised the whole situation. Being a people-pleaser, I hated confrontation; but I hated compromise even more. The delicate balance between grace for our leaders who disagreed so strongly with us, and the courage to act on our convictions was proving to be even harder than I'd imagined. How tempting it was to cast judgment when we felt we were right and they were wrong. Yet how painful it was to know that they—the leaders we loved and respected—were struggling in the same way. From the Rileys' perspective, we were heartlessly abandoning them in a lurch of nightmarish proportions. Everything was on the line.

In spite of our desires to handle the situation humbly and wisely, we did not handle it perfectly. Many a thought was *not* bathed in love nor prayer. We agonized, criticized, worried, and vented. We hurt. But ultimately, we had to let go. We strove to forgive perceived wrongs and extend grace, but we failed on many accounts. We longed to honor Jesus in the mess. But the battle against a new kind of cynicism had only begun.

It was time for the Cap Haitian expedition: eight to ten hours of stomach-churning curves and exhilarating cliffs. Once the nausea, headaches, and more Cedarmont Kids CDs than we could count were behind us, we gratefully made the acquaintance of Tom Froese's family. Just like us, he and his wife, Helen, had adopted two Haitian boys and one Haitian girl. However, unlike us, they'd chosen to raise these three kids after already raising their own three children to adulthood. I wasn't sure if they were brave or just plain crazy.

The Froeses currently rented the first and third floors of a newly constructed house (the second being rented by a Haitian family), each floor with its own staircase and entry. Tom escorted us to the third floor, where we piled our suitcases and gang into two stifling but spotless tiled rooms.

We spent the next few days swapping stories of our experiences in Haiti and sharing dreams for future ministry. Tom and Helen introduced us to Pastor Monestime, who led the church down their street. Our experience with "godly Haitian men" of late left us slightly skeptical that he was the "gem" Tom and Helen described him to be, but they assured us that Pastor Monestime asked nothing in return for the privilege of helping their newly founded ministry. They were impressed by his messages, his outreach, and his lifestyle. We assumed a wait-and-see stance.

A few days into our innumerable discussions on how to best help the children of Haiti, we were ready for some recreation. We remedied our restlessness with a day trip to the infamous Citadel, a stone fortress built by the sweat and blood of thousands of Haitians under the reign of Henri Cristophe, who declared himself king of northern Haiti in 1811.

The most regrettable decision of our expedition came at the start. Haitian horse masters swarmed like bees. "You must ride a horse!" they insisted, wagging fingers in our faces. "It's too far for your children. You'll become hot and tired."

We caved and paid their fees. It was a long, steep hike, after all. But only minutes up the three-thousand-foot mountain we realized our mistake. We simply could not adjust the Haitian-made stirrups to accommodate somebody taller than five feet—which all of the adults among us were. Additionally, we were soon tempted to reverse roles and carry our poor beasts of burden. Our guides rewarded them with nothing but curses and whips for all their efforts. Completing our shame and misery, we arrived at a parking lot halfway up the trail. We could have driven, saved money, and prevented the abuse of our horses had we only known. We received the physical payback for our folly later that night and over the next couple days, as every last one of our party received a first-class education on the term "saddle sore."

Our respite in Cap Haitian had removed us from our volatile TIH situation, but a seemingly unrelated scenario, at the forefront of every Cap Haitian missionary's mind, reminded us we were not out of the woods yet. While in Port-au-Prince we'd already heard some of Jim White's story, but here in Cap we learned more. Jim and his wife had ministered for years in the Cap community.

They'd recently prepared to welcome a new missionary couple who had sent a shipping container full of personal belongings ahead of their arrival. When Jim attempted to pick up the container, he'd known two guns would be among the goods—weapons that had already received proper clearance. What he hadn't known about was the gun powder, the ammunition, and a bomb-making instructional book. The customs officials and police accused Jim of terrorism, and threw him into a Port-au-Prince prison. President Aristide—known for neither justice nor mercy—seemed bent on Jim's destruction. No trial had been arranged.

Nothing was clear. The motives of the prospective missionary, the involvement of the police, the possibility of a set-up, just an unlucky misunderstanding. Anything was possible. But in a place like Haiti, these games and confusions could be deadly.

As Jarod and I pondered the consequences of "blowing the whistle" on Joseph's lies, our concern about his police-officer brother grew. Who knew how angry or vengeful the two of them might become if we revealed the extent of Joseph's corruption?

By the end of our visit to Cap Haitian, we knew we would be contacting the U.S. Kids Alive office. It seemed this was indeed our open window.

"We've got to get out of here." Jarod's seriousness startled me. Our trip to the States was coming up in about a week, but that's not what he was talking about.

"What? Now? We haven't been accepted by Kids Alive yet. Where would we go?"

"Jen, Joseph is furious with me. We have to get out of here as soon as possible. I'm not taking chances with you and the kids. This just isn't safe anymore."

He had my full attention.

"I'm calling the Froeses to see if there's a place we could move to in Cap Haitian before you and I fly to the States. We need to get far away from here, and quickly."

Jarod paced into the next room to make his call. I longed to hear the conversation, but his pacing made it impossible. Fifteen minutes later, he gave me his report.

"Tom says we're welcome to move all our belongings into the third floor of their house—where we stayed during our visit."

"Great!"

"And we can do it this week."

I just stared at him.

"Jen, I mean it. We've got to disappear. Tom is sending a driver with a truck the day after tomorrow to transport everything. We'll load his truck before the sun rises and be out of here before anyone can ask any questions."

We started packing as soon as Madam George left that afternoon. She wasn't scheduled to come the following day, so we used our privacy to complete the job. The only people informed of our flight to the States were the Froeses and the Cadets. The Cadets planned to babysit our kids the following week to facilitate the fertility tests in Florida, so the kids and I (along with our two dogs) would drive to their home while Jarod delivered our truckload of belongings to Cap Haitian.

Just over a year ago we'd unpacked and settled in. It seemed too short a time to form a family, learn a language, and leave a ministry. But here we were, packing a truck in the dank predawn air, my heart pounding and my mind spinning. As our departure and daylight neared, we called Madam George to break the news of our move. She came speedily for a tearful goodbye. She gratefully collected her severance pay, our reference letter, and accepted the news of a replacement job we'd already found for her. We bid our new guard, Matye, goodbye as well, leaving him extra money, assuring him we'd soon be in touch. He'd been a faithful worker—we would invite him to our new home once we were settled.

And that was it. Eager to put space between us and any danger, Jarod hugged and kissed us as we mounted our vehicle, then jumped into the truck with Ronald, a Haitian driver from Cap, for the winding journey to our new city. I was almost envious of their treacherous trip when I considered the mission before me: I was responsible to navigate Port's intimidating traffic and puzzling streets, then make the steep ascent up its surrounding mountains in our overheating Blazer, all the while fielding endless questions and questionable smells from three toddlers and two caged dogs. I found myself wondering, amid cries and yelps, if I'd ever before had a legitimate reason to call myself stressed.

I could have kissed the Cadets' gate an hour later, it was such a welcome sight. Relief was within reach. I slipped out of the driver's seat to knock. Pierre and Yvette were all the medicine my twitching nerves needed.

But an employee I'd never met opened the side door just a crack.

"Wi?" she said, waiting for me to state my business.

"I'm here to stay with Pastor Cadet and his family. They know we're coming," I said in Creole.

"Well, they're not home." She wasn't rude, just careful enough to seem aloof. "I can let you pull into the yard, but I don't have the right to let you into the house."

I felt my eyes grow wide as I pondered how long we'd be stuck, but tried to recover gracefully.

"Maybe I can call them so they can explain to you." I pulled out my phone and dialed. "See, I have three kids and two dogs in the car. . . ." But Yvette didn't answer, and I could see this woman wasn't going to budge.

"I'll just bring the car in." My shoulders slumped. I pulled the Blazer into the yard, and she closed the gate behind me. At least I didn't have to stay on the street. I continued calling Yvette, now with Daphne crawling all over me and Justin blasting questions in my ear. "Why aren't we getting out? Can we play? Where are our friends?"

I had no idea what to do with three kids and two dogs in a yard ruled by Tiger, the most ferocious canine I'd ever met. I thought I might be able to corral my little humans into a safe zone, but our dogs were another story. If I left them in the car much longer, I was afraid of accidents, not to mention suffocation in the heat. If I wrestled their cages out (easier said than done), their mere presence in the yard would tempt Tiger beyond what he was able to bear. Yes, Tiger was tied up, but the fact that his nature more closely resembled his namesake than any other animal on earth gave me very little faith in the ability of his rope to hold him back.

My new "frenemy" seemed to have disappeared back inside, leaving me to manage my dilemmas on my own. I thought I'd developed some measure of patience during the past year, but the tension of the momentous morning and the burden of *dogs*, no less, had me more than a little irritated at the nightmarishly slow speed at which time seemed to pass in this country. I was also irritated at this woman's lack of trust in my desperate report that we had indeed been invited into the Cadets' home.

My concern for our ridiculous pets in the back of our car finally drove me to regrettable action: I heaved their cages out, muttering bitterly at my beloved husband, who had assured me it was a good idea to take the dogs to the Cadets'. What happened next was exactly the worst-case scenario I'd prayed I'd avoid. Buddy, our bravest, most foolish dog escaped his confines and frolicked around the yard . . . no, frolicked around *Tiger's* yard, chased *Tiger's* chickens, peed on *Tiger's* territory, and dared to look *Tiger himself* in the eye. They both disappeared from view, Tiger stretching his tether around the corner of the house, and the air was soon filled with yelping, growling, scuffling, whining, and finally, whimpering. Before long, Buster limped back into view. He had a bloody limb, but my sympathy only went so far. He was lucky to be alive. So were we, for that matter. Thank God Tiger hadn't actually broken his tether, or we might all be limping.

Just as my spirits were about to crumble completely, Pierre and Yvette finally arrived. They were aghast that we'd been forbidden entrance, and when they properly introduced us to "the woman," her regret and humility helped me at least consider forgiving her. Yvette explained to me in English that she'd completely forgotten to tell her that we were coming and that she takes her job of "protecting" them very seriously. I couldn't imagine how threatening a wilting mother of three preschoolers could have appeared, but then again, with urchins like mine, anything breakable or clean was in imminent danger. There may have been some wisdom to her madness.

In a short time the Cadets and their workers had our dogs situated, our stomachs filled, and our hearts cheered. The only remaining strain of the day would be the uncertainty of Jarod's journey. Word had it that Haitian drivers could make the cross-country trip in about four hours—less than half the time it had taken us. I was already imagining the truck careening off a sharp turn, rolling down the cliff, and myself a widow, stuck forever in Haiti with unadoptable children, rabid dogs, and a tragic tale of woe.

Again, the hours crept by at the speed I would have driven to Cap. Once four hours had passed, my concern grew. I called Jarod's number again and again, to no effect. I called the Froeses to find out if they'd heard anything. When they sounded as concerned as I was, I began to panic in earnest. *What kind of Haitian driver takes more than four hours to make that trip?* Something must be wrong.

But my attention was diverted to more urgent matters. I heard a thud, a blood-curdling scream, then Justin's frantic chatter. I sprinted downstairs and outside.

Jaden's face was covered in blood. His forehead was twice its normal size, and the skin was completely scraped away.

"What happened?" I yelled at Justin.

"He was walking on top of that, and he fell down!" Justin said pointing to a ledge seven feet above the cement landing we were standing on.

I shuddered and wanted to vomit. *How was Jaden not dead?* Unbelievably, his limbs were all in working order, and his wails seemed to pertain only to his forehead.

I scooped up my miserable child and rushed him to the upstairs bathroom. Dabbing the blood away, I searched the cabinets for disinfectant. My only option: rubbing alcohol.

His screams pierced me to the core. Of all the stupid mistakes I'd made that day, this had to be the worst. My sympathy and admiration for the courage of my special little son rose to new heights that day. As did my blood pressure.

Once we had determined that Jaden would live and did not have a concussion, I got my brood ready for bed. We pulled blankets and sheets around the master bed that Pierre and Yvette generously gave up for me. I read a Bible story about trusting God, all the while nauseated by fear that Jarod was dead. We prayed, and as the kids drifted to sleep, I buried my head in my hands and let the tears fall.

"God, I can't do this! I just know he's dead, and I don't know how I'm going to make it. It's all just too much."

# 8

# Not What We Prayed For

Every good and perfect gift is from above.

James 1:17

As I finally collapsed on the bed, my phone rang. Through bleary eyes I recognized the Froeses' number. My heart thudded.

"Hello?"

"Jen, it's me. We just got to the Froeses' house."

I could finally breathe.

"Are you kidding me? I thought Haitians made the trip in four hours!"

"Not this one. Ronald seems to be related to the entire population between Port and Cap. We stopped to talk with *everyone*. I knew you'd be worried, but I had no phone reception."

I couldn't deny I was furious with Ronald but I was too exhausted and relieved to let my frustration out on Jarod.

"I've gotta go, Jen. Just wanted you to know I'm okay." I

thought he was done, but then realizing he'd forgotten something important, he added, "Did everything go all right for you?"

A short laugh burst out of my mouth. "Long story. I'll let you go for now though. Love you."

"Love you too."

For the whole twenty seconds before my mind and body fell into oblivion, I praised my God who had preserved and delivered us all.

He'd even had His eye on my dumb dogs.

Our tireless trio was safely secured with the Cadets. The whirl-winds they created merged seamlessly with the shenanigans of their newfound friends. Though the yard held countless chickens, the testosterone of seven young boys, two mischievous (though now confined) mutts and the wild-eyed Tiger, I somehow knew everyone would be fine. Pierre and Yvette had a spiritual gift for managing three-ring circuses.

Jarod and I sat on our American Airlines flight, reveling in cool air, iced Dr. Pepper, and in-flight entertainment that seemed ludicrously trivial. Our respite was bittersweet though. When we'd entered Haiti, we'd envisioned our next flight "home" to be the adventure of parents toting strollers, backpacks, and unruly kids.

"I wish they were with us," I said quietly. My mommy heart had already forgotten the spills, accidents, injuries, screams, and fits of the morning.

"Well," Jarod said, "this could be the trip that makes it all happen."

Again my thoughts turned to the subject of infertility. *Who wants to be proved infertile? This is ridiculous.* But my resolve was growing. I imagined returning with doctor verification and dramatically slapping it onto Madam Clerveaux's desk. The sooner we got it done, the better.

Though the fertility clinic was in Florida, just a short jump across the Atlantic puddle, we'd decided to fly first to Chicago. We'd already finished the bulk of the application process to Kids Alive International, and it was time for some interviews at the office in Valparaiso, Indiana. The timing of our U.S. trip was perfect.

We spent our first day on American soil driving to Valparaiso, meeting the KAI staff. After several interviews, evaluations, and forms, we headed back to Chicago. Joining Kids Alive was not dissimilar to an adoption process—extremely thorough. We weren't done yet, but were at least another step closer.

Three of our favorite couples, the Greenes, Marners, and Caffees, met us at Chicago's Palmer House that evening. I was transported back in time, back in Chicago haunts with old friends. From all outward appearances, things were just as they had been one short year ago. But out of sight did not mean out of mind. The tug of my heart reminded me how much had changed; that all that was most precious to me was now in Haiti.

We walked to Panda Express for dinner, to quench the craving for American-style Chinese food Jarod and I had endured all year. We glibly conversed in English, relishing the freedom to be loud and boisterous without receiving second glances from anyone in the restaurant. We blended in again.

Our friends plied us with questions, and I happily satiated their curiosity with descriptions of Jaden, Justin, and Daphne.

"Let's put it this way: If they were here right now, at least two drinks would've spilled, we would've made three trips to the bathroom, there'd be rice all over the floor, and I would have yet to take a bite."

But even if they were little tornadoes, they were also heartbreakers, personality oozing—or more like exploding—from every pore. I wouldn't have minded three trips to Panda Express's bathroom and pop on the floor so much. I just wanted our kids to be with us.

I pushed my orange chicken around on my plate as we talked. It didn't taste quite as good as I'd thought it would.

It was around midnight by the time my adrenaline had settled to normal levels and allowed me to fall asleep in our hotel room. And the alarm rang far too early for my liking.

We'd had a one-hour time change, an exciting but draining day of reentry into the United States, and a late night. I showered, dressed, and tried to force coffee into my sleepy, queasy system, mentally rehearsing what I'd say to the Edgewater Baptist congregation in this morning's missionary update. I skipped the breakfast muffin offered in the lobby since I was feeling a bit nervous.

Despite the morning's painful start, we were energized

by our supporting congregation. As we updated them on our past year and the purpose of our trip to the States, our friends assured us of their prayers. They'd already been praying for the adoption of our kids for two and a half years and were eager to see everything resolved.

Driving our rental car from Edgewater to the airport to catch our flight, Jarod pushed the speed limit. "I don't like driving fast anymore," I mused. "I forgot how pressured life can be in the States. I might be having some reverse culture shock." I suppressed a bit of pride in my ability to so wisely evaluate myself.

I could tell Jarod wasn't so sure.

"No really, I'm just overstimulated here. Too many billboards, flashing lights, TV, media. It kind of makes me feel sick. I bet I've just adapted to a slower pace in Haiti."

In classic American haste—which had never bothered me a day before in my life—we rushed our car to the drop-off, jogged to our takeoff gate, and zipped off to Orlando, arriving at last at our hotel. Thanks to a high-pressure time-share offer we hadn't been able to resist back in our first year of marriage, we were able to afford a week at a beautiful resort and deceive ourselves into believing we were enjoying a real bargain.

I was ashamed to admit to anyone how particular I was about hotels. It wasn't so much the cleanliness (though of course that mattered too) or the firmness of the mattress. No, if I didn't like the decor pictured online, I'd find an excuse not to stay there. Of course, I rebuked myself for this: *And you call yourself a missionary? What would Amy Carmichael or Elisabeth Elliot think of you?* But for this week, I would let myself be refreshed by our charming suite, multiple swimming pools, and miniature golf courses. Then I'd soldier on in Haiti, David Livingstone style.

We couldn't truly relax though, until we'd made our "business" trip. We had an appointment at a Fort Lauderdale fertility clinic, and so we had to catch a Greyhound bus before dawn. Early mornings and I have never gotten along, and as I fought stress, fatigue, and even a sick stomach the next morning, I vowed to sleep in and indulge myself as much as possible for the following five days.

A highlight of the trip was that Becky—a dear family friend who lived in Fort Lauderdale—was our chauffeur for the day. She taxied us between the bus station and clinic on her way to work, with the promise of food and lodging once our appointment was over.

And so we arrived, the moment of truth awaiting us.

*Lord Jesus, you know how badly we want to adopt our kids. Please work this all out for good.*

The office was filled with fashionably dressed women, and I felt a little out of place. The couples that could afford fertility treatments were clearly in a different financial bracket than we were. Of course, we weren't there for treatments. We'd come for rather the opposite reason.

After a one-hour wait and innumerable forms, I was ushered to the doctor's office, where I was asked to clarify my personal information. And she didn't just mean my phone number and address. Regular menstruation? Not really. Date of last cycle? Right now. Amount of time trying to conceive? Our past four years of marriage. Any known miscarriages? No.

Finally, she escorted me to an examination room where she

explained she'd perform an internal diagnostic ultrasound. From all appearances, we were there to catch a glimpse of a baby—mom and dad in the ultrasound room. But the children this ultrasound was for were already born, waiting for us in Haiti.

The doctor slipped the tiny probe inside me, and began her commentary on the images on the screen.

"Here's your right ovary. . . ."

*A sight I'd never really expected to see.*

"That looks fine. Now let's see the other one. . . ."

Once it too was pronounced in working order, she launched into an explanation of what she was looking for in my uterus. Then she held the probe still for a moment, and the tone of her voice changed.

"And this. . . . *This is . . . a baby!*"

The words exploded in my ears. But the doctor just rolled right along.

"Yes, it appears that you're actually pregnant! Congratulations! The calculations show it to be five weeks and six days old."

We were speechless. Then, finally, "Uh . . . thanks!"

"Wait, *what?*"

"*Really?*"

After only a couple minutes of wrapping our heads around this shocking information, the doctor set our minds spinning again.

"Now take a look at this: this is actually a blood clot that has formed around the baby. I don't want you to be alarmed. Everything will probably be just fine, but right now you believed you were having your period because your body is trying to get rid of the blood clot. This is considered a *threatened* miscarriage."

*"Pregnant"* and *"miscarriage"* in the same breath? "Can anything be done?" Now I was feeling nauseated.

"Yes, I want you to spend a week on bed rest. No lifting anything heavier than five pounds. I'll give you progesterone suppositories as well. With all of that, you will probably be just fine. The spotting should stop soon. If it starts again after you're back on your feet, just go back to bed rest again."

Her speech and the ultrasound were over. And just in time.

"I . . . I think I'm going to throw up. Is there a restroom nearby?"

She pointed down the hall, and I made a run for it. As I vomited into the toilet, I realized what my queasiness over the past few days had been. It wasn't exactly reverse culture shock. I had to admit I was beyond thrilled to hear that I was pregnant. This was something I'd barely dared dream of. But what if I kept bleeding? I stumbled back to Jarod and the doctor and collapsed on a chair.

"I think I'm going to pass out!"

After a glass of water and a few more instructions from the doctor, I was holding my own again.

"Well, give me a call if you have any problems in the next several days," the doctor said. "Good luck, and again, congratulations! I think my work here is done. I wish all our patients were cured so quickly!"

With that, we were dismissed. Our moment of truth had indeed come. And the truth couldn't have been any more surprising. Our adoptions were obviously back on hold, which truly disappointed us, but something so miraculous with such ironic—or serendipitous—timing could only be from God. And if He chose to place the gift of another child in our laps at such a time as this, He must have His reasons.

The rest of our day was spent shocking everyone we knew.

"Mom? Just wanted to call to let you know we're finished at the fertility clinic. No, we weren't able to get the papers we needed. Yeah, it is frustrating. But they just can't give you documents of infertility when you're not infertile. Well, yeah, if they discover you're pregnant, it just wouldn't be right to document infertility."

The long-awaited week, which was to have been filled with shopping trips, sightseeing, swimming, and romantic dates was a train wreck. I grew increasingly sick with each passing day, and became well acquainted with the walls of the bedroom. Jarod spent his days running errands—knocking out my Walmart list and catering foods I could stomach an entire bite of. As miserable as I was, jealous that Jarod got to have all the fun, I couldn't deny the sweet sovereignty of my heavenly Father in arranging this week of rest for me. Had we not traveled to the States for testing, I would have been juggling children, dogs, and the possessions we were in the process of moving—clueless to the fact that the health of my unborn baby was at stake. Little had I known how invaluable a doctor's appointment and this getaway would be.

Experiencing God's wisdom and goodness during a week of intensifying nausea and fatigue buoyed me up for all that lay ahead. There were some things I was aware I would face: Where and how to have a baby when our three Haitian children would not be able to leave the country with us; how to find a home in Cap Haitian; how to not overdo myself and put our baby in danger; and of course how in the world to ever adopt our three children. What I didn't realize was that an even bigger test of faith was just around the corner.

# 9

## Disruptions

He is not afraid of bad news;
his heart is firm, trusting in the Lord.

Psalm 112:7

As we ate our first dinner in Cap Haitian at the Froeses' house, Tom introduced us to the four-year-old boy they'd taken into their care. "Marvin will live with us until we can get our first children's home opened." Then Tom lowered his voice. "His mother tried to poison him, and there's no one else to care for him."

"What?" *Why would someone do that?*

"Yeah. She poisoned Marvin and his little brother and locked them in a shed to die."

I looked at Marvin, worried we would distress him, but then remembered he didn't understand English.

"A neighbor found Marvin, but it was too late for his brother.

People say his mom is crazy," Tom continued. "I'm sure it's got something to do with voodoo."

"So he's our first child for our first home," Helen said.

The home was the big project on the horizon. Even though Jarod and I hadn't officially been accepted by KAI, we'd been given permission to join the team and would soon be making ministry plans together with the Froeses.

Our kids—and, more amazingly, the Cadet family—had survived the past several days. We'd made the breathtaking drive from Port-au-Prince to Cap and were thankful for friendly faces and the upstairs apartment to crash in until we could find a rental home of our own. I was famished, nauseated, overwhelmed, and relieved at the end of this long day, but the Truth in Haiti cloud of intrigue was now behind us, and the future looked promising.

During dessert, our conversation shifted to politics, which in Haiti was synonymous with the topic of safety.

"Have there been many riots in Cap?" Jarod asked. "It's almost nonstop in Port right now."

"I'm sure it's not as bad as Port," Tom said "But, Aristide's gangs are here too. They block the roads with burning tires now and then."

President Aristide paid thugs to terrorize people and bribed the poorest neighborhoods with increased electricity so they would vote for him. The people in positions of power, who'd been so placed because of their connections to Aristide, were behind him as well. But the general population was quickly becoming disenchanted with their Catholic/voodoo priest-turned-president. Government corruption and bullying had never been worse. And when anyone protested, the *chimere*–his gangsters–responded violently. The country was simmering.

We cleared the table, then herded our overstimulated kids up the outdoor stairway to our third-floor apartment. The open windows let in the voices of Haitian neighbors as well as the distant voodoo drums. Always the drums. I was growing accustomed to constant noise, but the more I understood about voodoo, the less I could tune out the drums. Their pounding signaled the witch-doctors' invocation of demonic spirits. People surrendered their bodies to be inhabited by the spirits in exchange for a favor–success, health, a visa, money, a curse on their neighbor, the death of an enemy. In every corner of Haiti this night, children like Marvin were affected by the power of darkness.

*Please let us make a difference, Jesus.*

A visit from my grandparents was huge. I was so proud of them for braving a fourth-world country. Our gang had recently moved out of the Froeses' house and into a rental home, so Nana and Papa's introduction to our new way of life started with the steep, intimidating climb to our hillside house. The kids delighted in teaching them some Creole, sharing fresh-off-the-tree coconuts, and showing off the oddest feature of our home—our very own handmade merry-go-round.

Experiencing Haiti through their eyes led me to the realization that I'd made more adaptations than I'd thought. For their first meal, I served turkey sandwiches—nothing to be proud of back in the States, but quite an extravagance in Haiti, where cold-cuts were expensive and could be found only at a couple elite markets. Our family dove into the sandwiches, puzzled by my grandma's reluctance after her first bite.

"I don't want to hurt your feelings, Jennifer, but this meat is spoiled!"

My mom, who'd traveled with them, echoed Grandma's sentiments. "Jen, smell it. This just isn't right!"

In Haiti, there was no such thing as "rotten" meat. Women marinated everything in powerful citrus juice, spices, and salt to undo the damage done by hours in the open market. I hadn't adopted that process myself yet, but I had been scraping the bluish-green parts off my ground beef on a regular basis. There wasn't much I could do about today's turkey though. Neither marinating nor scraping would fix my dilemma.

I gave in to peer pressure and confiscated the sandwiches from everyone but Jarod and Papa. Jarod wasn't one to cave. And Papa . . . well, he was raised during the Great Depression. There was no way he was going to throw food away.

My grandpa, the ultimate carpenter and perfectionist, couldn't keep himself from inspecting our home as we gave them the tour. He shuddered at each angled wall, the slant of our "level" floor, the wiring, and the plumbing. When he and Jarod began their project of building a TV cabinet, his second day in-country, he set out to create not only the most square, level shelf unit in Haiti but also the most structurally sound, precision-made wooden sawhorses in the Caribbean. He was determined that *something* in this country should be made properly.

After a week of Papa's piggyback horse rides and Nana's

Bible stories, my grandparents were invited to dine with Pastor Monestime. The rice and beans and chicken feet—yes, feet—were the highlight of their stay. "After all," Papa said, "I grew up on chicken feet. We didn't waste *anything* when I was a kid."

The morning of their departure flight, the chimere were on the streets again. We'd begun to take them more seriously. We'd had a rattling incident just a couple weeks prior. During a visit from Andrew and Jamie Marner, our friends from Chicago, we'd dismissed concerns about a "crazy" man who harassed drivers on the way to church. As we neared his spot, he and a few other thugs blocked the road, forcing us to a stop. The kids, Jamie, and I sat quietly in back, while Jarod opened his window to reason with them. Reason was met with a swift punch in the jaw followed by the theft of his watch. I froze and prayed silently, wondering how ugly things would get in front of our children. In an instant, Jarod shook off his initial shock, shifted into reverse, and took us out of danger. We were fine, of course, but wanted no such incident with my grandparents.

Considering Nana's tendency to worry, Jarod would avoid the main road—the chimere's focal point—taking the rougher back route to the airport instead, where there wouldn't be any danger for them. But I couldn't help wondering how safe Haiti would be for anyone if this kind of rioting continued.

I pushed through the nausea that never seemed to leave me, tuned out my whooping children, and tried to focus on our meeting. Tom and Helen sat at our plywood table, sharing the news:

"Philip and Fifi Morency are interested in becoming house parents for our first children's home!"

Philip and Fifi had two young children of their own. Due to Philip's recent job loss, they were all living with Pastor Monestime's family. Pastor Monestime was recommending this couple for the job, but jaded as we were, Jarod and I had already voiced our concerns to each other that perhaps he was just eager to move them out of his house.

"Is there any way we can get to know them better before placing them in a position of such responsibility?" I asked.

The children that would eventually fill our homes would have many issues. Even the wisest, godliest, most educated counselor would be challenged by the task of parenting ten to twelve orphaned, abused, starved, abandoned, or unloved children.

"It would be nice to have some kind of trial period," Helen said.

We'd already had some discussions with Tom and Helen about how difficult it would be to find the kind of house parents we needed. Kids Alive International worked in many countries, and perhaps it was easier to find mature, even educated believers in some places, but the truth was, most well-educated Haitians had already found a way to leave their homeland. Godly, mature believers were nearly impossible to find, and faithful married couples were few and far between. Haiti was founded on a slave revolution in which African families had been torn apart from day one, a legacy that makes the preservation of family values, Christian virtue, or godly traditions difficult at best.

Jarod voiced the question we were all thinking. "How do we

know if they want to be house parents out of a heart for the Lord, or if they're just desperate for a job?"

"Well, it could be both," Tom said. "But if Pastor Monestime is recommending them, I'm willing to give them a try."

"I do like the idea of getting to know them better, though," said Helen. "Jennifer, I know you're not sure about getting house help, but what if you hired Fifi for at least a short time, to get a feel for her work ethic and character?

I looked at Jarod. "It's up to you, Jen," he said.

I quickly processed the pros and cons: on the one hand, privacy and freedom alongside endless chores and exhaustion; on the other, further cross-cultural stretching but somebody to share the workload. Who was I kidding? I was tired, and I knew the right answer.

"Let's do it."

Fifi had a chance to prove herself, and prove herself she did. She was hard-working, honest, and kind. By the time we'd grown accustomed to her help, we were ready to "promote" her. She and Philip became house parents.

⌘

I sat on our bed, paging through books on midwifery as Jarod shut the computer down for the night. "So, hon," I asked, "do you think you could deliver this baby if we can't find anyone else to do it?"

"Sure. You've got all the information we need, right?"

Jarod's confidence made me laugh. I would rather have him deliver our baby than go to the *Justinian*, Cap's infamous hospital, but I was still praying that Cheron Hardy could do it. Our nurse-midwife-missionary friend ran a local orphanage, essentially parenting about forty children. She hadn't delivered any babies since moving to Haiti the year before, but was praying for the opportunity to do so. She was younger than me, but had the confidence and maturity of my mother. There was no doubt I would have trusted her for our delivery—even without hospital backup. The only issue was her mission's hesitancy; from their perspective back on U.S. soil, the concern of a lawsuit outweighed my need for medical help. Thankfully, Cheron was at least allowed to provide my prenatal care.

Most, if not all missionaries traveled back to the States for the birth of their babies. It made sense; there were few adequate hospitals in Haiti, and besides, Haiti was just a short jump off the Florida coast. The majority of missionary families flew home each summer to visit supporters and relatives, so why wouldn't they make the easy trip back for something as eventful as a baby's birth?

We didn't have that luxury though. Our children weren't permitted to leave Haiti. If Jarod and I were to travel "home" for the birth, it would mean leaving Justin, Jaden, and Daphne in someone else's care for a couple months. I'd need to fly out a month before my due date, then wait for our baby's passport to be issued afterward. Even if we had felt comfortable leaving our children again (which we didn't), no one was standing in line to babysit. Had it been Justin and Daphne . . . maybe, but throwing little "Taz" into the bargain made everyone think twice.

There had to be another way. Maybe I could have the baby in the Dominican Republic. Or maybe Cheron would be allowed to do the delivery. Or maybe Jarod *could* do it. I would keep praying. There were still a few months for the Lord to put everything in place. I returned my attention to my midwifery book, but Jarod interrupted.

"So Jen, I hear there's an army forming right now in Hinch."

"*Army?* Does Haiti even have an army?"

"They were disbanded in the 1990s, but they seem to reform themselves when they want to plan a coup."

"You think they're planning a coup?"

"Oh, I'm sure someone is. I think there's always someone planning a coup in Haiti. The question is, can they succeed?"

"Do you think there's anything to worry about?"

"There probably is for the people supporting President Aristide."

"And for us?"

"I don't think so. Nobody is opposing missionaries or Americans."

We kept our eyes and ears open over the next days, as did the general population. Smiles faded, conversations were hushed, eyes darted. No one wanted to reveal whose side they were on. Life experience had already taught them to keep a low profile and trust no one. Few were willing to stick their necks out. In Haiti, their necks might get chopped.

"The army is on their way to Cap," Tom announced in our living room. It wasn't matter-of-fact news. He looked troubled. "Most missions and NGOs are pulling their people out."

"What? Why?" I was confused. "Isn't the army just passing through to get to Port?"

"They are, but they'll probably stay to gather supplies and more soldiers. And they'll target Aristide's guys—the chimere and the police force."

"But why are Americans leaving?" I still didn't get it.

"Well, the entire police force is going to be missing indefinitely."

"That means chaos," Jarod said. "There's no telling what will happen if there are no police."

"So are you thinking of leaving?" I said, not even wanting to consider the possibility for Jarod and myself.

"Helen and I are talking about it. We're going to ask Pastor Monestime what he thinks. You guys should talk about it too."

"We can't leave our kids!" I whipped my head around to look at Jarod, sure he would agree. "If all the missionaries are leaving, there's no one to take care of them!"

"Well, of course, this is totally up to you guys, but Helen and I wondered if maybe Philip and Fifi could stay in your house and care for your kids if we all have to leave. We would leave Marvin with them as well." Tom stood up and walked to the door. "I've gotta go. Jarod, maybe you and I could go talk to Monestime together a little later."

Jarod nodded and said goodbye to Tom while I sat reeling on the couch. This just sounded so wrong. Who'd ever read a story where the missionaries "did the right thing and *left* their work and children to run for safety?" Surely God wanted us to stay.

"We need to take this seriously, Jen," Jarod said the next day.

"Pastor Monestime says our kids will actually be safer without our conspicuous white faces around them."

"Are you kidding me?"

"No. He meant it. He thinks it would be wise to have Philip and Fifi move into our house. They'll blend in with everyone else; they won't be a target." He paused. "Plus, I need to take care of you. You're six months pregnant. Cheron Hardy already left, and there's no one here to help you if anything happens."

A horn honked outside our gate. I knew it was Tom and Helen, come to continue the discussion on evacuation.

Matye, our guard who had moved from Port to Cap to work for us again, opened the red metal gate, holding our dogs by the collars to keep them from escaping our yard. In a few minutes, our kids and the Froese kids were spinning the merry-go-round and the adult conversation moved into the living room.

Tom cleared his throat, then began. "I've communicated with the KAI office about evacuating. We're all in agreement that the best course of action would be for us to fly to the Dominican Republic."

Helen said, "We wouldn't be far away, it's not too expensive, and best of all, we could tour the Kids Alive children's homes and schools of Jarabacoa. We could learn a lot."

I was a little relieved. I wouldn't be too far away from my little ones. We could come back the minute it was safe. Maybe it would only be a few days.

"When are you thinking about leaving?" Jarod asked.

"As soon as possible. Maybe tomorrow or the day after." Tom looked at us as if to ask if we were in.

"We don't know how long the airport will be operational," Helen said. "We need to buy our tickets soon to be sure we'll make it out in time."

My adrenaline surged. I had a lot to do.

"So you all really think we need to do this?" I wanted to hear it one more time.

Tom and Helen nodded, and Jarod spoke. "Jen, I really don't want you here under these conditions, and our kids need to be safe. I think the best thing we can do for them is to leave."

"I can bring Philip and Fifi over so you can show them the ropes," Tom said. "And Jarod, we should go buy our tickets."

I tuned the rest of the conversation out. I knew we had to do this. I didn't have much choice with everyone in authority over me insisting this was the wisest decision. But how would our kids understand? How could three children who'd been left in an orphanage be "fine" with adoptive parents who kept disappearing? We would try to explain to Justin, but would a five-year-old who'd already been abandoned continue to be resilient through more changes? And could Jaden and two-year-old Daphne possibly grasp any of what was going on?

Tom and Helen left, and my swirling thoughts and I jumped into dinner prep. Thank God the kids had already become acquainted with Fifi. *You knew what you were doing there, didn't you, God?* I spread flour on the table and rolled and cut my biscuit dough. Justin would be thrilled to have Marvin staying in the house; they were good buddies. Marvin had picked English up quickly from living with the Froeses. I wondered if he and Justin would keep the English rolling, or switch back to Creole. Jaden's vocabulary was a total hybrid of languages. His speech impediment made both languages equally impossible to understand. It would be up to Justin to translate for him, which was a sort of hit-or-miss operation. Daphne didn't talk too much yet, probably because of the clash of languages in her overwhelmed little brain. Who knew what would come out when she finally did talk? She could sing though. And humming right on pitch worked in any language. *Lord, how long will we be gone? What am I going to miss? And can I just ask why they couldn't have been adopted by now?* I felt like a horrible mother. I should have refused to leave.

But as I shoved the pan of biscuits into the oven, a kick from my womb reminded me that I had another child to think about as well. I didn't have any real fears that anything would happen to this baby if we stayed, but Jarod felt so responsible. He wouldn't take the chance.

I washed the flour off my hands with a heavy sigh.

The day had come. We would fly out in the afternoon. I glanced at Daphne in the car seat beside me. She was all smiles and babbles as we drove to the Froese's house on an errand. My stomach was in knots. Today things just *weren't fair.* Why did our adoptions have to be at a two-year standstill when others (who *weren't* facing evacuations) had easily been adopted in less than one year? Why did our age or fertility matter when that of countless others did not? Why wasn't there some way to bring our kids out of Haiti?

Tears began to fall down my cheeks. I turned the radio up to keep Daphne from hearing me cry. But soon the tears flowed even faster. The 4VEH station, echoed by my musical daughter, seemed to bring a message straight from God's lips: "God is in control."

And so, as our plane—the very last flight allowed to leave Cap Haitian—lifted off the runway several hours later, I wept tears of both longing and relinquishment. Yes, I hated the brokenness that separated Jarod and me from the kids who needed us, but our kids were in His hands. He was in control.

# 10

## A Dream

Wait for the LORD;
be strong, and let your heart take courage;
wait for the LORD!

Psalm 27:14

My head knew we'd done what we had to, and God was in it. But even so, when I turned the facts over in the darkness of the Dominican Kids Alive guesthouse, they haunted me. This was real. We'd actually left our kids behind. This was not the stuff missionary biographies were supposed to include. The stories I'd read extolled the courage of those refusing to abandon the war-torn countries in which they served. Like captains who go down with their ship, missionaries—not to mention *mothers*—were supposed to risk everything for those they loved. Panic crowded out the peace I'd rested in only hours before. *What was I doing here? Why should I be safe in these cool Dominican mountains when the ones dearest to me were at risk across the border?*

The choice had not been mine to make; but had I fought hard enough?

I squeezed my eyes tight and blew out a conflicted sigh, careful not to wake Jarod. *Jesus, really? Is this what you want?*

There was no audible answer, just a flashback to the heartbreaking beauty of my little girl, singing in the front seat of our car. Warm tears ran down my cheeks as the memory faded, and I nodded in the quiet bunk room, giving my kids to God for the hundredth time that day.

I was human. I couldn't make the promise never to leave or forsake, no matter how passionately I wished I could.

But Jesus already had.

A couple days into our Dominican stay, we found a phone center from which we could call Philip, Fifi, and the kids since our Haiti cell phones didn't work across the border. We spoke with each of them, relieved to hear normalcy in their voices. Justin's chatter of escapades with Philip and Fifi's children helped put me at ease. Life for him was still about toys, friends, and the small things that were supposed to fill a child's days, at least from what I could tell.

"How are you, Justin?" I asked, wishing he could verbalize more than the "fine" that he knew was expected. "Are you having fun?"

"Yes. We're riding bikes. I'm playing with Marvin." He sounded so young over the phone. "When you gonna come home?"

My heart sank. My answer wasn't going to make either of us happy. "I don't know, Justin. We can't come yet, but we're praying we'll be able to come soon. You have fun playing with the kids. Help take care of Jaden and Daphne, okay?"

"Okay."

"I love you."

The following days brought discouraging news; not only were endless travel advisories in place for foreigners, there were simply no flights. The fighting was only escalating. But even while my heart was in Haiti, I carried my fourth child with me.

*How do I plan for my baby's birth when I don't know where I'll be in a few weeks or even months?* Thus far my only considerations had been a home birth in Haiti or a complicated trip to the States. But maybe the Dominican was a third option worth pondering.

"Would you recommend giving birth in the D.R.?" I asked a Kids Alive missionary as she drove us around Jarabacoa.

"Absolutely," she said. "The capital has great doctors."

The next day, Jarod and I toured a birth center in Santo Domingo.

It was beautiful—the facility boasted cozy suites and up-to-date technology. The obstetrician performed a prenatal checkup and showed openness to my natural childbirth philosophies. My brain buzzed with possibilities the whole bus ride back.

"I'd love to give birth in a place like that," I said, sighing, once we were back inside our tiny cabin. Jarod and I squeezed ourselves and my growing belly onto the bottom bunk, and I rolled my eyes at our ludicrous sleeping arrangements. Back in the heat of Haiti, bunk beds or even the fifties-style separate-beds-for-married-couples arrangement might not have been a bad idea, but here where temps dipped into the sixties and where my heart was aching, there was no way I wanted to fall asleep by myself.

Jarod interrupted my mental rabbit trail. "But having the baby here still doesn't solve the issue of our kids."

"True," I said, "but this isn't as far away as the U.S." Still hopeful, I continued thinking aloud. "I could come on my own before the due date, and you could leave the kids with someone and possibly make it in time for the delivery."

"Even if I did happen to get here in time—which is doubtful—I just can't imagine leaving them again so soon. And who knows how long it would take to get the baby's passport and paperwork?"

Jarod was right. My visions of the comfy birth suite and capable medical staff—visions of safety and security for my baby and me—burst like the fragile, elusive bubbles they were.

"I can't either." The reality stung. "I can't imagine doing that to our kids."

Our exile lasted four weeks, the last two of which we spent in the States. The comforts of family, friends, and first-world luxuries took the edge off our pain, but when we received the email from Tom that we'd been given the green light to return to Haiti, the tears that blurred the message on the screen were tears of joy.

We flew back into the Dominican Republic, then met a friend at the Haitian border. As he drove us back to our Cap Haitian home, and we took in the evidences of trouble, including the burnt-out airport, I still didn't have answers. There was no undoing the past month. But at least I could move forward. My family would be together again.

"Mommeeee . . ." Justin's voice rang of older brother right-to-tattle tones. "Jaden's eating dog food again!"

He dragged a guilt-ridden Jaden in by the arm.

"Jaden, no! Spit it out!" I held out my hand to receive the dribbly, grainy chunks of dog food. "Gross."

I ran to my one-basin kitchen sink to clean off. This happened too often, and it was getting old. "We talked about this before you went outside, Jaden."

He'd created his own little mantra. It was a grammatical mess, but he used it to tell himself what not to do: "No water dog! No food dog!"

"Why don't you listen to yourself and stop doing this, buddy?" Of course answering that kind of question was far beyond his ability. Maybe my child needed more salt. Or a chew toy. Or maybe supervision. I swung Daphne on my hip and stepped out into the sunshine with the boys. It was only nine in the morning, but the air was thick. I was thankful for my lightweight yellow dress—the coolest piece of clothing I owned. Even so, I knew I would reek by afternoon.

"Jaden, come ride your bike!"

He spun in a circle—his classic Jaden move—then sat on the tricycle. He attached his crippled left hand to the handlebars and prepared to push off with his feet.

"No, Jaden. Use the pedals."

He flashed a look at me, then grudgingly obliged. I knew I was spoiling his fun. He could zip around the yard at near light speed if he was allowed to use the trike as a scooter, or push with his feet. The pedals were just a nuisance he delightedly avoided.

"Good, Jaden. Now go down the hill." Once the slope propelled him forward, his feet absorbed the pedaling motion. Jarod and I were convinced he'd eventually catch on from this neat little trick and be able to pedal on his own. But what a typical child might pick up in ten tries, Jaden might learn only in three hundred. We were probably somewhere in the two hundreds.

"Hey Jaden!" Jarod called as he stepped outside with an armload of paperwork. "Are you using the pedals?"

"Wi!" Jaden was all business, eager to win his Daddy's praise.

"Good job, buddy!" Jarod said, then turned to me. "I've got to take these papers downtown. See you all later." He climbed into the Blazer. Matye, hearing the car door slam, came out of his two-room dependans to open the gate for Jarod. I corralled the kids while Matye held the dogs by their collars.

Just as the white cloud behind the Blazer billowed away, I turned to find Jaden lying on the ground.

"Jaden? What's going on?" It took a few seconds for me to realize he was having a seizure. I knelt down beside him, thinking it would soon be over; but the seconds continued to tick by.

"Matye, watch him!" I opened the door of our gate and sprinted into the Blazer's dust trail, wildly hoping Jarod might still be in view. No such luck.

I ran back to Jaden, sprawled stiffly on the cement. "Honey, are you okay?" He was completely rigid, his eyes rolled to the side. His breath came in shallow gasps, and as I rested my hand on his chest, the rapid fluttering of his heart frightened me even more.

Matye held Daphne, and Justin, for once shocked into silence, stood by.

"I've got to call Jarod!" I grabbed my cell out of my pocket, desperate for my husband's advice. But though Haiti's phone companies could easily put cells in our hands, quality service was still greatly lacking. Neither Jarod nor Cheron Hardy were reachable.

*God, what am I going to do?* I cried silently as I cradled Jaden's head. My thoughts jumped to the American missionary doctor, Mark Pearson, who lived at the bottom of our hill. Since we were still relatively new to Cap, I'd not yet met him, but it was clear he was our best chance for help. *Please, Jesus, just let him be there!*

"Matye, stay here with Justin and Daphne. I'm taking Jaden down the road to the doctor's house."

I hoisted Jaden's unbending frame over top my seven-month-pregnant belly and stumbled down the rocky path. Again, I was a spectacle, alternately jogging and skidding past neighbors shuffling along on much slower missions. I might have found help, had I thought to ask, but I was too frantic to think clearly. I didn't slow until I reached the Pearsons' gate.

I shifted Jaden and pounded on the door, trying in vain to wipe the sweat from my eyes with my shoulder. *Oh please God, let him be home!*

Dogs barked inside. Struggling to free my hand to knock again, I kicked at the door. Finally it opened, revealing a white man and two Dobermans. "Are you Dr. Pearson?" I said, practically attacking him. "My son's having a horrible seizure. Can you help?"

Dr. Pearson grabbed Jaden out of my arms and swept him into

his living room, a makeshift clinic with plastic tubs of medical supplies and a couple beds.

"Has he had seizures before?" He placed him on a mattress, then dug through a drawer of vials.

"Yes, but nothing like this. They're usually over in a minute or less." I watched him load a syringe.

"Is he on any kind of medication?"

"No." *Should he be? Was this my fault?*

"Okay. I'm giving him a shot of Valium, which should slow everything in his system way down. We should see the seizure end almost instantly."

He swabbed alcohol several inches above Jaden's scabbed knee and injected the valium into his thigh.

"And if this doesn't work?" I panicked as the seizure showed no signs of stopping.

He watched Jaden carefully. "I'm giving him a second injection. This will definitely do it." I dialed Jarod's number again, adrenaline fueling irrational anger at Jarod for not knowing what was happening. Still nothing. But as I hit the "End" button on the phone, Jaden relaxed and began breathing normally again.

I sank onto a chair in relief, and Dr. Pearson took off his glasses, wiping sweat from his face.

"What was that?" I ventured. "Could he have...*died?*"

"A grand mal seizure can be dangerous, depending on how long it lasts," he said. "The important thing is that we stopped it. Now we'll need to work on preventing any more."

"So, he should be on medication?"

"After today, yes. We don't want to see this happen again."

I shuddered. *No, I sure don't.*

Thirty minutes and a successful call to Jarod later, we were in the Blazer, headed back up our hill. The ordeal was over, but "what ifs" churned in my mind. *What if Dr. Pearson hadn't been there? What if the Valium hadn't worked? What if this had happened at night when we didn't know?*

"That was so scary," was all I uttered, letting my head fall against the window for a moment of rest. We hit a pothole and the window knocked me away with a vengeance. I massaged the pain away, wishing I could rub away my fears as well.

"I'm so sorry," Jarod said as I closed my eyes. "Thank God for Dr. Pearson. . . ." His voice trailed off as he too pondered what could have been.

But Dr. Pearson had been there and had exactly what we needed. God had placed us on the same mountain, knowing we would need him—this moment, this day.

God knew. He always knew. "What ifs" were pointless. But this wouldn't be the last time I asked them.

I ended the call and looked at Jarod. "This might be our answer!"

"The doctor sounds good?"

"Yep. He was educated in the U.S.—Mayo Clinic no less. He speaks good English, and he sounds pretty easygoing about my desire to do things naturally."

"And his fees?"

"Here—look." I'd written everything down, and showed Jarod the figures. This doctor in Port-au-Prince was more affordable than anyone in the States or the Dominican Republic. And of course, giving birth in Haiti meant our family could stay together. We'd probably have to fly to Port—I didn't want to bump and jostle the baby out prematurely on an eight-hour drive. But, even with the expense of our thirty-minute flight, we would do better in-country.

"What do you think: We fly to Port a few weeks before my due date, my mom flies from the States and meets us there. Then we stay in the guest house at Baptist Haiti Mission and wait for me to go into labor. When it's time, you and I drive down from the mission to the hospital in Port."

"Could work. And you know there's a hospital at the Baptist Mission too—if your labor goes too fast."

But that wouldn't be my problem.

"What are those horrible sounds? Those women sound like they're *dying!*"

Our guest house was a mere coconut's throw away from the mission hospital's maternity ward.

The "dying" women were giving birth. It was prime baby season. The screaming continued day and night.

My heart went out to them. I wished I could share the wealth of childbirth knowledge I'd acquired in recent months. Not understanding the natural course of the process had to make their pain worse. From what Cheron had told me, most young women possessed very little accurate information on conception, birth control, and pregnancy, let alone childbirth.

All my research kept my mind on the straight and narrow during the day, but when the wailing echoed through the still mountain night, it wasn't as easy to fight the doubts tugging at my soul. *Was that woman okay? Should I have thought longer about the Dominican birth suites?*

And then there was Jarod's recurring dream, the one he'd had since high school—the little blonde girl, running through a meadow, his daughter, whose mother had died. I tried to shake it off. After all, everyone has eerie dreams every now and then. And my faith wasn't built on dreams.

But the cries were hard to block out. Were any of those women slipping away, leaving motherless daughters? Life was as fragile as the Haitian hibiscus blossom—delicate and daring in its beauty, but gone in one fleeting day. Death was no respecter of persons, no matter how much education one had.

Our initial meeting with Dr. Charles was successful. Logistically complicated (lost taxi, long walk, whiney children, sweat and tears), but successful (we found the doctor). He, unlike my very American self, was not impressed by my lack of weight gain. He insisted my stomach was measuring too small—an ultrasound should be performed to determine if the baby was healthy.

Thankfully, the Baptist Haiti Mission clinic offered ultrasound services performed by French nurses. The fifty-something nurse scanning my belly attempted to make conversation in French. I was unable to understand most of what she said, except a few words that were identical in Creole, one being "girl."

My stomach flip-flopped. "You know I *don't* want to know

the baby's gender, right?" I asked in Creole, wishing I could undo what I'd just heard.

"Oh!" She made a valiant recovery effort. "Then you won't want to hear what I just said about your little boy."

*Nice try, lady.* A smile pulled at my mouth. A girl! Then my heart skipped a beat. *A little blonde girl?* The image Jarod described of our daughter in the meadow flashed in my mind.

But the nurse interrupted, now speaking Creole to make sure I understood. "You need to have this baby very soon. You don't have much amniotic fluid left, and your placenta is aging." She raised her eyebrows. "You need to ask your doctor to be induced."

I was horrified. All my natural, holistic, hippie midwifery books were completely against induction. It was a slippery slope. I was sure a healthy, normal body like mine would deliver when the time was right. After all, "childbirth is a natural process, not a disease." But Dr. Charles hadn't received my midwifery memo. At the news of my "aging" placenta and low amniotic fluid, he gave me two days to go into labor on my own. "But no longer."

Twenty-four hours later, I shifted my weight from one foot to the other in the bank's winding line.

"I can't believe we almost forgot about this." My husband—Mr. Crisis Prevention—was kicking himself.

I avoided eye contact with the dozens of curious bank patrons, instead keeping my gaze on the kids as my mom did her best to entertain them.

"I never once thought about cash for the hospital," I said.

"Well, I should've thought of it earlier." Jarod wasn't letting himself off the hook yet. "I'm sorry we all had to ride the taptap down here again."

I didn't want to make him feel any worse, but the taptaps were actually pretty high on my list of things to avoid. I was weary of the body odor, personal-space invasion, and bemused glances. But our hour careening down the mountain was over. We were here.

As we reached the front of the customer service line, I noticed out of the many tellers exactly one working quickly and with a smile. Of course, it wasn't our teller.

"Wi?" Her glare told me we'd offended her just by showing up.

"Bonswa. We need a cash advance from our American debit card, please," Jarod said.

Exhaling loudly, the teller pressed the phone keys with her fake red nails.

*She looks like she stepped straight out of the U.S.*, I thought as I surveyed her braided extensions and makeup. But I knew all her careful grooming had taken place on a dusty street corner where she'd slapped mosquitoes away and fanned herself with a rag.

She clunked the phone back in its cradle. "You have insufficient funds."

"What?" Jarod and I said together, faces blank.

"You were denied. You don't have the funds."

That was embarrassing to hear in any language in any bank.

Once outside, a panicked and pricey call to the States enlightened us to a "time delay" (up to two weeks) of our online records that we'd failed to take into consideration—ever. The money on our computer screen was no longer with us.

Our gloomy visages alerted my mom to a wrinkle in our plans, though neither of us could actually bring ourselves to put the matter into words. Feeling like idiots, Jarod and I whispered and muttered for the next couple hours, trying to devise plan B. *Should we have the baby at the Baptist Mission? In our apartment? Would the local doctor help us?*

Finally, my mom broke into our miserable privacy. "What's going on, guys?"

The confession was bitter on our tongues, but it yielded a surprisingly sweet fruit: "Well, if all you need is cash for the hospital, let's go back to the bank tomorrow and get a cash advance on my credit card."

"Really, Mom?"

"Of course."

After an early-morning trip to the bathroom, I felt it. Contraction number one. *Oh joy! Oh wait, no! It's Saturday, and we have to go to the bank before anything else happens! I'll just calm things down and go back to sleep. This will take forever anyway.*

I did fall back asleep, though I stirred occasionally as my belly tightened. By morning I was on the fringe of true labor, but nowhere near the thick of it.

By eight o'clock, Mom and I were bumping knees, elbows, and shoulders with strangers in the back of a truck as we made our way back to the bank. An hour later, gravity and a ride on a pothole-ridden road all the way back up the mountain had jostled my baby a few centimeters closer to delivery.

This bank trip paid off. We managed to obtain funds *and* not have a baby doing it. Something finally went as planned.

Saturday night, wasn't at all restful. My contractions came every ten minutes—annoyingly endurable yet also unignorable. I dozed for a few minutes between each one.

Sunday, I determined to walk my baby out into the world. I walked the trails in the woods, the paths by the missionaries' homes, the steep incline to the BHM gift shop, bakery, and restaurant. I even walked the main road, looking for a pharmacy that might sell castor oil. No one had a clue what castor oil was, but my contractions did finally intensify. Late in the afternoon, Jarod and I hired Jeff, BHM's taxi driver, to take us to the hospital.

Mom assured us of her prayers, and the kids bubbled with excitement.

"We'll be back soon with your little sister . . . or brother," Jarod promised.

The first sign that things would be challenging was the complete indifference of the hospital staff. We'd called Dr. Charles on our way, and while he assured us that he'd be there eventually, he seemed far more interested in finishing the *sermon* he was about to preach. He instructed us to tell a nurse to give us a room.

We did our best, but the nurse wasn't impressed with this chain of command. "The doctor must be here for us to give you a room." She was emotionless. "You see those people?" she said leaning her head toward the assortment of people in a waiting area. "They need rooms too."

Our eyes widened. This was the "best" hospital in Port-au-Prince. Things looked clean enough, but the whole "no room" thing was eventually going to become problematic.

I kept walking. The last thing I wanted was a stalled labor. But after several laps around the waiting area, I became aware of everyone's stares, then wished I hadn't. A dozen smart-aleck comments ached to slip off my tongue, but I knew I'd either fumble them up and embarrass myself, or else regret my rudeness. I couldn't blame people for staring. A friend had recently told us that Haitians almost never see white women pregnant. In fact, someone had asked her to clarify—"Do white women have babies and nurse them the same way we do?" Since most missionaries and expats travel back to their home countries right around the time they are becoming "large with child," someone like me was indeed a rare sight. There I was, pacing, bending, breathing heavily, closing my eyes, and *not* screaming. And white. I couldn't have been any stranger.

Hours passed. It was dark. I was not as interested in presentation as I had been at first. I was tired, not happy, and very ready for a room.

Finally, our preacher arrived. Dr. Charles was still reveling in the beauty of his sermon. He smiled as he loosened his tie and beckoned us down the hallway to our room. I tried to be forgiving, but could tell Dr. Charles had failed to start the night on Jarod's good side.

"All right! Here you go. You can turn on the air conditioning and change your clothes. I'll go change, and then we'll see how soon this baby wants to come."

The baby didn't show signs of wanting to come any time soon.

Hour after hour, Dr. Charles would knock, enter, and check again. "Hmmmm. No progress." He'd shake his head gloomily and promise to be back in an hour. Soon, I was convinced our baby was retreating from his knock. I didn't know how I could be in so much pain for so long with "no progress."

How I wished for a patient hippie midwife to walk out of my Ina May childbirth book and reassure me my baby would come at just the right time. "Don't try to rush things or get impatient. Your body knows what it is doing." I believed the midwives. I just wished Dr. Charles did.

By around five in the morning, Dr. Charles's impatience grew. He pulled the fetal monitor out to prove my baby was in distress. Jarod kept track of the heartbeat along with the doctor. It was still in the safe range, but Dr. Charles insisted it was borderline. He urged us to consider a C-section, which we firmly declined.

An hour later, I was at my low point. I hadn't screamed, cursed, or cried, but I was exhausted—wiped out beyond ability to reason coherently. When Dr. Charles came with the stethoscope and yet another announcement of "no progress," I caved. After months of Ina May, after giving dissertative speeches on the evils of the cesarean, I buckled.

"I'll do it." I said.

Every bit of color left Jarod's face.

Dr. Charles smiled and patted my hand. "We'll be back in a minute to prep you."

He motioned for Jarod to follow him out of the room, and I lay back on my bed, sleep mercifully claiming me between contractions.

A few minutes later, I awoke to a thud.

Turning my head, I looked for Jarod. Seeing no one, I closed my eyes again. But several minutes later, a figure slowly rose from the floor.

"Jarod? What . . . what were you doing?"

He was pale and unsteady. "I, uh, I think I fainted."

"What? Why? What's wrong?"

With tear-filled eyes, he reminded me of his dream. "Jen, please, don't do it. Don't let them cut you open. I can't handle the thought of losing you. Please just hang in there. You can do this!"

Even while I begged him not to think of his dream, fear's tiny seed was planted. *What if he's right? What if this is it?*

I swung my legs off my bed and stood to face him, leaning on him for support. "Jar, I'm so sorry. I just can't do this."

I laid my head on his shoulder. *How would Jarod care for four kids without me—a special-needs child and a newborn? Being trapped in Haiti by corruption as a complete family was one thing, but for him to endure the loss of his wife? God, surely you wouldn't let that happen!*"

I finally prayed aloud. "Please Jesus, help us trust you and not be afraid. Please protect us and give us wisdom."

Jarod just held me. I knew he still disagreed with my decision.

"Let's not talk about the dream anym—" I began when the door burst open.

It was Dr. Charles, ready to suck any last glimmer of hope we might be clinging to. "We must transfer you to *l'Hopital Rue Berne* in order to be prepared for anything. We're afraid for your baby."

Jaden, Daphne, and Justin in Port-au-Prince, 2002

Cap Haitian, 2006

Dora and Daphne riding through Cap Haitian

Christmas 2006

Playing "Restaurant" in the front yard

Thanksgiving feast with our deportee friends, 2008

Christmas 2008

Kids Alive Christmas Meal, 2008

Paradise Beach, November 2009

Haiti's National Palace after the Port-au-Prince earthquake of
January 2010

Jarod loading supplies for the post-earthquake relief effort

Media interviews in Miami after arriving in the States,
January 22, 2010

Welcomed to Wichita, Kansas by the Jordan/Litke family,
January 23, 2010

Welcoming Jarod to the States after the relief work
was handed over to Samaritan's Purse

On the family farm in Kansas, June 2010

Officially a family after nine years of waiting!
Harvey County Courthouse on our children's adoption day,
September 20, 2010

Jarod's parents celebrating "Adoption Day"
with us in Newton, Kansas

Life in South Florida, 2012

Florida, August 2015
Justin, Dora, Jennifer, Jarod, Brendan, Jaden, Daphne,
and Jaden's seizure dog "Beauty"

# 11

## Charrier Days

The testing of your faith develops perseverance.

James 1:3

MAY 17, 2004

Things were spiraling out of control. Dr. Charles instructed us to gather our belongings and prepare to leave shortly.

As soon as the door shut behind him, Jarod exploded. "This is all about money!"

"Why do you think that?" I really wanted to be able to trust my doctor, but Jarod's faith in him was long gone.

"This is ridiculous! Don't you see it? He insisted the C-section was to "save" our baby. He convinced you that our baby is "in distress," because then he can perform a C-section, which earns him far more money than a regular delivery. Now that he got you to agree to it, he is *fine* with delay! If this was really an emergency to save our baby, you would be on the operating table right now!"

"But why does he want us to transfer?"

"I'm guessing he's got friends at that hospital. Why not let them in on the money too?"

My foggy brain was in no position to reason at its normal capacity, but I had to admit Jarod had a very good point.

We changed, packed, and waited.

Dr. Charles finally opened our door and gave instructions. "I want you to take the flight of stairs over there, then walk out to the parking lot. You'll see the nurse by my car. Wait for me there."

Jarod and I looked at each other again. *Walk? Stairs? Car? Wait?*

The term *transfer* had stirred images of wheelchairs and ambulances. But I'd forgotten where I was.

There was no choice. I stumbled down three extensive flights of stairs, leaned on Jarod for another four hundred yards to the parking lot, then stood by Dr. Charles's two-door box-on-wheels until he meandered over to join us.

We drove several miles at a jogger's pace, then wound our way to *L'Hopital Rue Berne*. I flopped out of the car in time to field a powerful contraction—providing memorable entertainment for the passersby of Rue Berne.

As fate would have it, L'Hopital Rue Berne's elevator was not in working order, and therefore, the third-floor maternity ward would be accessed . . . by stairs, naturally.

I was assigned a gurney and dressed in a hospital gown. After Dr. Charles explained we'd commence upon the arrival of the surgical assistant, he disappeared. Half an hour later, Jarod hunted him down. He'd had enough.

"Dr. Charles, you insisted our baby was in distress. You

talked my wife into a C-section. You dragged us to a second hospital where we'll have to pay extra. The least you could do is pay attention to my wife and our baby. You haven't checked our baby's heartbeat for almost two hours, and this was supposedly an emergency!"

We received expert care for the next several minutes, until the assistant appeared.

*My last chance*, I thought, wracked by contractions. *Jesus, would you please help me to have this baby naturally?*

And then I felt the answer to my prayers.

"Dr. Charles," I called out, hoping he was nearby. "Dr. Charles?"

"Yes?" He walked in and gestured an attendant to push my gurney. "We're off to the operating room."

"Wait. . . . Dr. Charles, I think I'm ready to push."

"Nine and a half centimeters!" he announced after a quick exam. "Let's wheel you to the delivery room!"

I pushed for an entire hour. Our child, or the doctor, or Eve, or whoever, was just *not* going to make things easy for me. But I couldn't deny that God Himself had ordained every moment of the day thus far. The delays, the transfer, the stairs, perhaps even lies: they were all a part of it. They were *all* in answer to our prayers.

And at ten o'clock in the morning, Monday, May 17, 2004, Dora Jane made her appearance in Port-au-Prince, Haiti. I was inclined to believe Jarod's conspiracy theory when our "fragile" child tipped the scale at eight pounds. No emergency equipment was deemed necessary.

And her mother was alive and well to take her home the next day.

I awoke in my Cap Haitian bed to the sound of many children. Perhaps there weren't as many as the noise level might indicate, but even so, I was instantly overwhelmed. Dora was crying for her morning diaper change and feeding, Daphne was crying because she was being bullied by a certain pair of twins, and . . . come to think of it, everyone was crying.

I thought back to the emotions and fears of delivering Dora just a few weeks ago. I'd prayed to *live*, prayed for the privilege of raising my daughters and sons; prayed for the blessing of a daily earthly struggle.

Here it was—my struggle.

*Thank you, Jesus.* I meant it. I was still overwhelmed. Still tired. But I was still grateful that Jarod's dream had not come to fruition. I had the opportunity to live, to live and to serve the God who amazed me with His wonders. I was beginning to know this God of mine a little better these days. It was one thing to hear the stories of God's faithfulness from my mom and grandparents. It was one thing to study theology and missiology, and even to fill my head and heart with Scriptures. But it was breathtaking to discover how *real* my God actually was. He loved me enough to *act* on my behalf. He heard my little prayers and pleas. He saw my dilemmas and took the time to show me His hand and His loving concern. My love for Him was growing.

And so I plowed through another sticky day with my beautiful, crying children. And on this day, I'd have the chance to grow my faith even deeper still.

I fed and dressed the kids, cleaned our breakfast mess, mopped up almost-made-it-to-the-toilet puddles, then loaded everyone into the Blazer for our ministry meeting. Jarod attempted to start the car, but clicks, groans, and pops told us we wouldn't be going anywhere today.

The fact was, we wouldn't be going anywhere in the Blazer for a number of days—our finances simply couldn't accommodate the necessary repair job. Despite a few monetary gifts from friends and my mom's help with the cost of Dora's birth, our bank account was a quiet, lonely place. Transitioning from one mission to another had left a few givers in the cracks—either forgetful about the change, or gone on to support other endeavors. We'd managed to feed our brood decently so far, but we'd also dug for change in the cracks of our couch and car seats just to buy some eggs before our next paycheck.

The Froeses drove up to our home for several subsequent meetings, but the day came when we decided to just make the walk over to their house. It wasn't far for an adult, or perhaps not even for a child, but our kids did their best to make the walk as complicated as possible.

I strapped Dora on with a Snugglie baby harness. Jarod carried Daphne, and we prodded Justin and Jaden along. Of course Jaden found walking in a straight line impossible. His tendency was to swerve directly *into* the path of oncoming traffic, regardless of the size or speed of the vehicle. We darted back and forth across the road, taking turns saving his life from reckless drivers and irritated pedestrians. Justin blasted commands to Jaden, kept a running commentary on the trash in the road, and asked as many theological and scientific questions as possible. Despite the challenges, we marched on. Until advice starting flying our way.

"Hey, *Blan!*"

The term irked us to no end. The literal translation was "white," but Haitians used it to include foreigners of any color. One of our typical responses was to turn it into a joke with a point: "I'm not white. I'm cream-colored." They'd typically chuckle, and we'd continue, "Would you like to be called 'brown' or do you prefer 'sir' or 'madam'?" Sometimes they got it.

"Blan!"

I let it go this time. "Wi?"

"Your baby is in the sun!"

"Yes, she is."

"That's not good! She'll catch a cold! She needs a hat."

*Seriously? A cold? A sunburn, maybe, but a cold?*

"Thank you." I was just going to move on and laugh about it later with Jarod. But Jarod was in the mood to educate.

"Actually, madam, did you know that the sun is good for babies?" he said.

She was intrigued.

"Yes," he continued. "White babies need lots of sunshine, or else they turn yellow. The sun gives everyone vitamin D, which is very healthy. Every baby should spend time in the sun."

"Oh!" She was a little stumped. "Mèsi." She turned to her companion and they talked the whole episode over as they continued walking. "Did you hear that blan? He says the sun is good for babies."

Jarod and I looked at each other and rolled our eyes.

"Next time, I'll put a hat on Dora," I said.

My chance came soon.

"Jen, we're going to have to walk to church today."

I groaned, fully aware that any protest was pointless.

Chaos ensued, but we eventually headed out the door with four children, two Creole hymnals, Bibles, and yes, the promised hat for baby Dora.

Not two minutes down the road, it began.

"Blan! You're carrying your baby like that?!" The woman pointed to my Snugglie carrier and smirked.

"Yes, I am. It works well."

"But your baby is in the sun."

*Ha ha! I am ready for you, lady!*

"Yes, she is! But you see, she has a *hat* on!" I triumphantly pointed out Dora's cute little bonnet.

"Yes, she has a hat," she admitted, but then she looked at me and waved her finger in admonishment. "But that's not enough. You must protect her from the sun with an *umbrella!*"

I gasped. How dare she one-up me.

"I give up," I yelled at Jarod as soon as she turned off the path. "I will *never* be able to do things right in this country!"

The drums. Always the voodoo drums. No matter where we lay our heads, we fell asleep to their tune. "God is stronger, but Satan is faster." With cultural beliefs like that, business was booming for witchdoctors everywhere.

I had almost succeeded in exchanging the drums for the peace of sleep when a woman's scream pierced the darkness. I bolted upright. The scream was followed by a crash—like the sound of furniture hitting a wall. More screams.

"Jarod! Do you think we should do something?"

"I don't know." He was slipping into flip-flops and rummaging for a flashlight.

"Do you think that woman is being attacked?"

"I'll go on our roof and see."

"Well, hurry! If I was screaming like that, I'd want someone to help me!"

He grabbed his light and sprinted up the stairway to our roof. I didn't have to follow to hear him.

"Hello!" he yelled. "What's going on?"

Our neighbor—the man of the house—yelled back, "It was a *chat mawonn*."

*A brown cat? What did that mean?*

"Chat mawonn?" Jarod yelled back.

"A bad spirit. My wife saw it, but I threw our oven, and it ran away. We're fine now."

Not long after, Jarod had his own demonic confrontation to ponder. Walking through the open market in search of fruit and vegetables, he found himself face-to-face with a "zombie," a man drugged by a witchdoctor and buried alive, then "resurrected" to do the witchdoctor's bidding—forever brain-damaged, forever controlled. Both Jarod and I had seen the man in town before—barefoot, ragged, hair so caked with dirt it was almost blond. His presence was unsettling. He turned vacant eyes at Jarod, muttering unintelligibly. Jarod broke eye contact, his gaze falling on a crude

176

dagger in the zombie's hand, pointed straight at Jarod's belly. The man closed the last few inches between them, and though the only logical reaction was fear, Jarod realized this man had no authority to touch him. The Holy Spirit's whisper swung the man aside like a door on a hinge, allowing Jarod to pass by unharmed.

Satan's grip in Haiti is real. The country was dedicated to the devil himself upon its inception over two hundred years earlier. The fruit of that commitment is evident at every turn.

Yet we found ourselves shielded by Someone greater.

"Mommy, Jaden smells like gas!" Justin said as I washed the boys' hands for lunch.

"You mean like the gas we put in the car?"

"Yes."

I leaned close to Jaden and sniffed.

"Oh my word. You're right. It's coming from his mouth!" I pried his mouth open and sniffed again.

"Jarod! Come here!" I dragged Jaden into the living room to find Jarod.

"This boy's mouth smells like gasoline! What should we do?"

Jarod took a sniff and then paled.

"Oh no. I had a cup of gasoline on the porch. There were nuts from our inverter batteries in it—I was trying to clean off the corrosion." He plowed through the door and tore through the junk on our porch.

"Here. I put the cup right here, behind this plywood so the kids wouldn't get into it!"

But the cup—currently holding dry nuts and bolts—now sat in plain view.

"Justin did you pull this out?" he said, holding the cup.

"No!"

"Jaden probably found it himself and thought it was juice." *Can gasoline kill a person? What do we do?*

"How could he drink that? It had to taste horrible!"

"Jarod! What are we going to do?"

"Call Cheron, she'll know."

I tried. But the phones of Haiti, as always, conspired against me in my emergencies.

"There's no answer, Jarod. And I happen to know Dr. Mark isn't in-country."

"Okay," Jarod said, his mind racing. "Okay, I'm almost certain he should drink milk."

"Well, we need to be sure!"

"I'm pretty sure. Don't we have an emergency book somewhere around here?"

We'd had one on top of the fridge before we moved, but of course now that we needed it, it was missing. I rummaged through stacks of mail and other papers.

"Jen, let's just give him milk."

*Oh God, please give us wisdom! Don't let us do anything stupid!*

I mixed whole milk powder into a pitcher of filtered water, while Jarod kept trying to reach Cheron.

I poured a cup for Jaden, and we watched him drink.

"I think he's supposed to drink as much as possible," Jarod said.

I gave him a second cup. It went down a little slower.

"Give him more, Jen."

I grimaced. I wasn't sure *I* could have drunk that much milk at once. "Are you sure? He's gonna be sick!"

"This could be a matter of life and death, Jen. We've got to water down the gasoline." He redialed Cheron's number as he spoke.

Poor Jaden angrily sloshed a little more milk down the hatch.

"The phone seems to be working!" Jarod said with his cell by his ear.

"Cheron? Hey! Uh, we need some help. . . ."

He hung up a minute later. "She said we did the right thing. He needed milk—he should be fine."

"Thank God!" I hugged Jaden.

"Yeah . . ." Jarod paused. "She said one or two cups would have been plenty." He patted Jaden's head. "Sorry, buddy."

Jaden finished the day with no further signs of distress. The only effect his beverage of choice seemed to produce was, ironically, a little gas.

The Kids Alive Haiti (KAH) objective goal was to buy land, build children's homes, and educate and disciple kids. Tom and Pastor Monestime spearheaded the effort to purchase property, but meanwhile rented a home on the Froeses' street for the Morencys' growing "family." Jarod and I trained Philip and Fifi as best we could, drawing from Scripture, from positive role models, and from the vast Christian parenting resources available in English.

Because quality Creole materials were so scarce, our regurgitated information was completely new to them. While I'd been skeptical that anyone raised in Haiti would be qualified to mother children with such deep emotional and spiritual scars, I had to admit Fifi exceeded my expectations. She rose at four each morning to prepare food, iron school uniforms, and braid the girls' hair. She rarely opened up to me (vulnerability was a trait she carefully avoided), but there was no doubt she was diligent, loving, and patient.

The Morency home quickly expanded—there was no shortage of needy children. As one newcomer completed a routine medical checkup—required upon entry—the little boy was found to have the early stages of a deadly virus. Another day or two could have meant death, but the intervention of the staff spared his life. Even the problems we couldn't see were in the hands of an Almighty God.

More children in Philip and Fifi's home, the beginnings of a school, land surveys, and talk of a second children's home meant more meetings and more work. I pushed to keep up with my responsibilities—house-parent training lessons, board meetings, curricula, parties, and outings, not to mention my own family. I began to feel the strain.

*Lord, show me how much to do and when to stop,* I prayed. *And some help would be nice.*

Summer brought a partial answer to my prayer. Sarah Smith, a fellow graduate of both my beloved Berean Academy in Elbing, Kansas and Moody Bible Institute, came to help both me personally and Kids Alive. I plunked responsibilities into her lap with gratitude, and she took them on with joy. As she left Haiti at the end of the summer, she promised to do everything in her power to move back for a longer term after graduation. I did not object.

About the time stress and exhaustion threatened to overtake me, supervisors from Kids Alive Canada came to visit the field. There was something about Cybil's sympathetic eyes that opened up the reserve into which I'd been stuffing all my junk. I let fly my frustrations of living in a different culture, my longing for a good listener, and of course, how much work it took to simply *exist* in a place that did not provide running water, reliable electricity, dependable phone service, or convenience foods.

I dwelt particularly long (unnecessarily—she did have eyes) on the challenge my own children provided.

"Do you think you'll have any more children?" she asked kindly.

I wasn't sure if there was a right or wrong answer in her opinion, but I already knew my answer. "Oh, Cybil, if I was to find out I was pregnant again I think I would just sit down and cry!"

Then I added, "Plus, I wouldn't know what to name the child. We've already got two J's and two D's. I'm not sure where to go from there."

A few days later, my eyebrows lifted off my forehead as two pink lines formed on the white stick in my hand.

I ran into the kitchen and handed it to Jarod. His mouth formed the word, "Wha . . ." while I sat down and cried.

# 12

## An Ever Increasing Load

Oh that you would bless me and enlarge my border.

1 Chronicles 4:10

Beni swa le nom d' Senye
Beni swa le nom d' Senye
Beni swa le nom d' Senye
Ki anwo

We sang and clapped our hearts out on our rooftop. This wide, flat space served as our Laundromat, our passion fruit vineyard, our kiddie pool platform, and our worship center.

The setting sun saturated the clouds with pinks, purples, and reds. Mosquitoes buzzed and poked, which tended to break the magic of the moment, but we stayed as long as possible to avoid the smoldering heat indoors.

Jarod slapped bugs off both his own and Dora's limbs. I laughed at Jaden, as he closed his eyes and danced backward, clapping with the rhythm of the song. It was one of his favorites.

> Blessed be the name of the Lord
> Blessed be the name of the Lord
> Blessed be the name of the . . .

"JADEN, NO!" Jarod screamed.

I jumped up, suddenly seeing the danger, but it was too late. Jaden had just danced himself right off of our roof.

Everything blurred. I waited for the sickening thud, but heard nothing. Jarod shoved Dora into my arms and ran downstairs. I gasped and begged God for mercy. Justin and Daphne ran forward to peer over the edge of the roof, but I yanked them back from sharing Jaden's fate.

"We're going downstairs," I ordered, shutting the roof's door behind us as they descended.

I didn't know if I wanted to find out what had happened or not. I held Dora in our living room and prayed, delaying the inevitable.

Finally I heard Jarod outside our porch.

"He's okay, he's okay!"

I could breathe.

"He's bleeding pretty bad, but I think he's going to be fine. Bring some towels."

As I ran for towels, Jarod brought him inside.

His face and arm were covered in blood, but as Jarod described what had happened, I realized it wasn't as bad as it looked.

"You know the razor wire around our neighbor's wall—right by the edge of our roof?"

"Yeah?"

"Well, Jaden's arm and ear got stuck to that. As he fell, the razor wire caught him, flipped him right side up and brought him down to the ground in slow motion. I saw the whole thing."

I was speechless.

I held a towel to his ear. Sure enough. The cartilage had a large tear at the top, but besides that and the wound in his arm, he seemed to be whole.

"I'll drive him over to Mark or Cheron to see if there's anything special we need to do about his ear," Jarod said.

He stopped for a second. "I think we just experienced a miracle tonight."

All I could do was nod with my hands glued to my cheeks.

Then he added, "Not many people can say, 'Razor wire saved my life.'"

I looked at the women around me through teary eyes. Words couldn't describe how much I appreciated and admired them. They'd all been missionaries in Haiti longer than I, and here they were, gathering around me at this week's prayer meeting, praying God would extend grace for the loads "they couldn't imagine carrying." I was quite confident they'd all carried burdens and responsibilities I would've wanted no part of, but I was not about to turn away their empathy or intercession.

Lucy Hess, veteran missionary of over forty years, thanked God that Sarah Smith would soon be coming back to live with us and prayed for us to find a bigger home to accommodate our growing household. When she lifted her white head with a final "Amen," she said, "You know, I may have just the place for you."

Several weeks later, Jarod and I listened to Jean Louis's offer in disbelief. I looked past him at the enormous two-story home we were discussing, recalling the tiny, awkward, costly homes we'd already scratched off our list.

Our options were dwindling, but since this beautiful home, recommended by Lucy Hess, had stood empty long enough to serve as an easy target to thieves and hooligans, Jean Louis was ready to strike an irresistible bargain.

Jarod stuck out his hand to accept the offer. They shook on it, and Jean Louis said he'd have the rental agreement drawn up downtown.

*God, you are too good to me!* I was in awe. The words of Luke 12:48, "from everyone whom much has been given, much will be required," rang in my head. *I promise to use this space for you. Help me be hospitable and share your love here.* It was a bargain to which I'd be held.

The house had seven bedrooms, an expansive kitchen, three full bathrooms, and additional rooms that could be used as living space, offices, dining areas, or bedrooms. The grounds held a dependans with four small bedrooms and a storage room, a tiled decorative fountain (why, I did not know), two fenced-in garden plots—one with a swing set, and a large cemented yard surrounding the house. Not insignificantly, there were also coconut, mango, lime, orange, grapefruit, avocado, and papaya trees scattered throughout the yard. As was the norm, everything was walled in by cement blocks rising to a height of nine feet, topped with bits of razor wire and jagged glass shards.

To be sure, this house was not quite the equivalent in quality as it was in quantity. Peeling paint on ceilings and walls indicated a flaw in the construction of the roof's drainage system; kitchen cupboards held an odor indicative of mice and cockroaches, wooden door frames bore evidence of termites, and bathroom showers, tubs, toilets, and sinks would forever be yellowed. Caribbean-style slat windows would remain open, inviting dust, noise, and the occasional breeze.

No, this was no resort, despite its size, but its tiled floors, ample yard, and numerous rooms were a blessing I was humbled to accept. Sarah would live in the three-bedroom section off to the side of the kitchen downstairs, and our family would use the upstairs bedrooms. We still had far more space than we needed, but I figured I'd let God fill it up however he saw fit.

We moved in that summer. Sarah was due to arrive in a few weeks, and our baby boy (I *asked* the nurse the baby's gender this time) was due in a few months. Things were lining up nicely. Cheron Hardy had actually been approved by her mission to deliver my baby if a backup doctor could be found. Then as if on divine cue, Dr. Steve James and his wife Nancy moved back to Haiti after a five-year absence. The only glitch in my birth plan was the unavailability of an emergency C-section. The nearest hospital (twenty minutes away) would not be able to provide anesthetization even if we did make it there in time for a cesarean. I was still mindful of Jarod's dream and entertained a few doubts and fears about all that could possibly go wrong, but even more compelling was God's undeniable provision and faithfulness. The only alternatives that covered every "what if" involved a long absence from my Haitian children. No, if God was able to provide a doctor and a midwife for a home delivery, I was convinced I could trust Him as we all did the best we could.

I couldn't wait to meet my baby boy. I was ashamed of my initial reaction to news of his existence. It wasn't that I didn't want him even in that first moment—it was just such a shock in one of my life's weariest moments; I still considered Jarod and myself relatively "infertile," I was nursing seven-month-old Dora, and in addition to all that, we were trying *not* to get pregnant. It was definitely unexpected.

But even after I'd cried, I'd laughed at the irony of my vehement declaration to Cybil. God seemed to enjoy dropping babies in my lap when I least expected them. I wasn't sure how many *more* times I wanted him to try this, but I had to admit, he was two-for-two with the element-of-surprise thing. With all the odds against my babies' conceptions, it was pretty clear that He wanted them around.

So did I. And I couldn't wait to experience my first home birth, come October.

"Mommmmeeee!"

There was a time back in Chicago when I would've given anything to hear a precious little voice calling my name. Now I was lucky if I made it two minutes without someone screaming for Mommy.

But this was the truly urgent version of the call. I dropped the carrots I was peeling and ran outside.

Justin was running toward me. "Mommy! Jaden hit the bees' house!"

"What?"

"Jaden had a stick and hit *all* the bees' houses!"

"You've got to be kidding me."

And then the screams erupted. I ran to Jaden as he rubbed his face and arms with his good hand. I grabbed him up—again over a large belly—into the house.

"Why do you *do* these things?" I was nearly weeping as I realized how miserable he was.

All he could do was cry and writhe. He was completely covered in welts. The "bees" were actually wasps, and they had exacted their revenge.

*Please, God, don't let him be allergic to their venom!* I could only imagine how short his life would be if he was.

"Justin, go find my phone."

Once again, Jarod wasn't home. I would try to call Cheron for advice. In the meanwhile, I'd try out some home remedies.

But Jaden was in such agony, I couldn't even leave him to find any cures. He screamed as if engulfed in flames. *That must be how hell feels.*

We paced the halls while I cradled and comforted him, praying for relief. When that didn't settle him, I'd lie him down on a bed.

When my call to Cheron finally went through, she recommended Benadryl. I soothed, sang, prayed, and rocked him

for the next hour until the medicine escorted him to uncon-
scious relief.

Mary had helped out a few times in our Charrier home. Her
employers were leaving Haiti, so now that I had even more floors
to mop and Jarod's workload with the KAH school was increas-
ing, I decided to hire her a few days a week at our new place. She
helped me cross some chores off my list, but things soon got complicated. The smiles I had no problem eliciting turned to scowls
when Jarod entered the room. Our once contented guard Matye
became mysteriously demanding after hushed conversations with
Mary in the backyard. On the days I needed Mary most, she'd
either arrive late or not at all, and without apology. My nonconfrontational nature recoiled at the thought of letting her go, but it
seemed to be my nonconfrontational nature that Mary was intent
on taking advantage of. By the time she demanded a raise and
talked Matye into demanding the same, I was no longer willing
to pay someone to add to my stress. Though I knew letting her go
was the wisest move, I was not immune to the sense of guilt—be
it real or false—that comes from being in a position to so affect
another person's life.

Mary responded in a rage. Though our severance pay was more
generous than the law required, she threatened to sue. It came to
nothing, but I hate letting people down. And being let down.

Kids Alive Haiti had just been disappointed as well. With
the help of a few lawyers from Pastor Monestime's church Tom
had purchased a plot of land for the mission. But to everyone's

horror, the mission found they'd been deceived by the seller: The land was already owned by another, who was fiercely unwilling to part with the property. As usual, the money was nowhere to be found.

The mission decided to file a lawsuit.

Sarah arrived in time for the storms. Hurricanes battered the already bruised country. Our home was perfectly situated on the mountain to be out of harm's way, so we had no personal fear of winds or rain, but the stories of death and loss overwhelmed us. The city of Gonaives was hit the worst. It always is. We couldn't understand why a town had been built in such an inopportune place. Floods were forever consuming it. Waters engulfed the town, help was cut off, and people died by the hundreds.

Haiti is the land of "why"? Why such brokenness? Why such destruction? Why such corruption? Why such spiritual and physical poverty?

But "why" wasn't nearly as hard to answer as "how"? How can we bring life? How can change happen? How can we make true disciples?

There had been hundreds of missions and humanitarian efforts in Haiti. Why hadn't they been able to turn things around? How could we do any better? These were the things we talked about nonstop, that consumed us. We prayed. We talked. We read. We researched. We worked. And we dreamed.

One thing we did know: Change would only come through the children.

"Hmmm." I paused with the plate of rice in my hand. "I think things are starting to pick up a little." I handed the plate to Justin as my mom and Jarod looked at me and my tightening belly with raised eyebrows.

"Nothing too intense yet, but maybe we should call Cheron and Dr. Steve and alert them."

"I'll call them." Jarod jumped up from the table and ran upstairs to get his phone.

"Really, hon . . . let them know it could be a while. They don't need to rush," I called after him.

Memories of Dora's traumatic birth pushed at the edges of my mind, but confidence in my competent friends overruled. This would be different. I let my mom supervise the kids in the dining room while I stood in the kitchen and took a couple bites off my own plate. Sarah was preparing her own meal, since she loved cooking for herself. Avery Davis, a young woman in her twenties, was there too. Avery was a guest to our home for several weeks while she assisted at Cheron Hardy's orphanage. Neither Sarah nor Avery were sure what to expect with my impending home birth.

"Are you okay?" Sarah asked.

"Oh yeah, this isn't bad at all," I said. Then I set my plate down and held on to the edge of the table to relax my way through another contraction.

"You're sure you're fine with me being present for the delivery?" Avery asked.

"Definitely. It's already going to be Jarod, my mom, Dr. Steve, his wife Nancy, and Cheron. What's one or two more? It'll be a party!"

"C'mon, Sarah. You've got to come too." Avery was delighted to witness a home birth, but Sarah staunchly insisted she'd rather babysit or do some other helpful task. She'd even considered going to another home while I gave birth. She couldn't stand the thought of hearing someone in agony.

"Sarah, I promise; I'm not going to scream," I said laughing at her, but stopped to let another contraction do its job.

"Well, I'll think about it." She watched me carefully. "If it keeps going like this, I might be able to handle it."

It *was* a party. And thankfully, the party was short and sweet—a far cry from the drama of my first delivery. Sarah's curiosity got the best of her. She stepped in our room and couldn't make herself leave until Brendan Clark arrived at eight in the evening on October 25th. No J's and D's this time around. "Brendan" was in honor of my mom—Brenda—and "Clark" was Jarod's dad's middle name. And with all grandparents duly honored in the names of our children, we believed five children just might be enough.

And the more loudly my beautiful baby boy protested the evils of colic, the more convinced we became.

# 13

## Breaking Points

Make haste to help me,
O Lord, my salvation!

Psalm 38:22

I wasn't sure if I was human or machine. Everyone needed me desperately. And so I ran. I rushed, darted, dashed, sprinted from one emergency to another. No time to feel, no time to process, and most definitely no time to relax.

"Jaden is bleeding!" *Apply Band-Aid, mop floor.*

"Mommy, mommy, MOMMY! Look at this spider!" *Move Justin away from the tarantula.*

"Mommy, I'm hungry." *Get Dora a snack.*

Hold Brendan when he begins to cry. Remember that the laundry needs to be hung out. Carry his bouncy seat into the shade and work.

A knock at the gate. *I'm sorry, Matye is not here right now.*

"Mommy, I'm hungry." "Me too." "Mommy I want to eat." "Mommy, food!" *What to do with chicken and rice today? In five minutes. While I nurse Brendan.*

Jarod comes home in search of our electric bill receipt. Electricite de Haiti is trying to make us pay a bill for the previous five years when we've only lived in our house for five months. Rummage through the desk I put it in months ago. *Where is it?*

Now it's raining. Rescue the laundry. Brendan is screaming again.

Where's Daphne? There, standing in a puddle of my favorite lotion.

Jaden needs a fifth cup of water, and a third trip to the bathroom.

Brendan can wail till I have a chance to burp him.

Justin's begging to watch a movie.

Lay Brendan in his crib.

Out to start the generator. Add gas, spill gas, check the oil, fight with the pull cord.

Run back inside to begin the who-gets-to-pick-out-the-movie negotiations.

I could feel myself steaming ahead to a full-on breakdown, but it was a runaway train and I had no idea how to apply the brakes. All I could do was shovel the coal and try to maintain control.

All the while, stories of kidnappings filled the air. We told ourselves it wouldn't happen in Cap Haitian—it was just a Port-au-Prince thing. Ruthless gangs stalked the wealthy, whether Haitian or foreign. They'd kidnap them, demand a ransom, and often torture victims to speed payment. The problem was, it worked. Every ransom paid reinforced the system.

And then it came to us; first a missionary, then a businessman's son, a teenage girl, a teenage boy. Ransoms were negotiated, releases arranged. We rejoiced when our missionary friend was unharmed and returned to his wife, but we all wondered how to handle the risks with which we lived.

Tom and Helen felt strongly that ministry routines ought not be broken in submission to threats. Jarod believed we should exercise wisdom and caution by changing routes and schedules. He also insisted that should he ever be kidnapped, no ransom should be paid. Tension was high, and everyone had an opinion on safety.

But as word of kidnappings ebbed and flowed, news of break-ins rose consistently.

Along with other neighborhoods, our own neighborhood, Mombin Lataille, seemed to be under attack. Everyone had a story. Robberies. Rapes. Beatings. I tried not to hear the details. I just trusted that our wall, our dogs, our guard, and our fortress-like house would be enough to intimidate thieves. The chances were pretty good they'd already passed us by.

But then our night came: the night I wished a 911 call could cross the Atlantic and bring real help.

*Is this it?* I wondered as I heard the men downstairs. *Is this the night that will redefine our lives? How will I handle it? God, give me grace!*

Sarah was in our upstairs bathroom, praying. Our kids slept, but I was terrified they'd awaken any moment to the sound of a true nightmare. Jarod knelt by the metal door at the top of our staircase, holding the can of gas. I stood in the shadows of the hallway, a knot of pain in my stomach, my hands gripping each other as if to keep my body from falling apart.

The footsteps on the stairs told me the padlock on the ground floor had been a joke to these men. They'd claimed to have a gun—even promised to shoot Jarod upon entry. Would they charge the steps and see how easy it was to reach through the openings above the door?

But the darkness was slowing them down.

*Who's going to make the first move?*

Jarod peered through the crack between the door and the wall. He saw the candle in the leader's hand and seized his opportunity. He poured gas under the door, letting it slosh its way down the stairs before picking up the matches.

This time the gas needed no explanation. The man holding the candle froze, then extinguished his flame. Instead of charging, he turned his back and ran down the stairs to the backyard. Gasping with relief, I moved toward my husband. But he was on the offensive now. He unlocked our door and jumped past the slippery gas puddles, his words trailing behind him: "Can you clean this up, Jen? Then lock the door again."

As I mopped the gas with towels, I heard Tom arrive, along with his son and our friend John. Soon spotlights filled our yard. The guys searched every corner, but it was too late. The gang had escaped over our back wall.

Matye emerged from his room just as the situation calmed.

Why had our guard remained silent for the duration of the event, and why had our two dogs "just happened" to have been blocked off from the backyard? We'd never know for sure, but fear was Satan's tool of choice here—the thieves had likely used it against Matye before the attack, and we knew they'd counted on it for their previous victims. Tonight it had worked against them, despite the voodoo protection they'd purchased. I was a mess, and I'd have my own fear to deal with in the days ahead, but I felt like I'd just watched David defeat Goliath with a measly sling and stone. "Saul's armor"—our guard, our dogs, our wall, our many locks—hadn't kept the enemy at bay. It wasn't by might nor by power we'd been spared—it was God's Spirit. Trembling and exhausted, I praised God the attack was over.

But Satan wasn't quite ready to give up.

Jarod jumped out of bed and reached for his ringing phone. "Tom? What's going on?"

I sat up, pulse instantly racing.

"I'll be there as soon as I can." He hung up and threw on some clothes.

"What is it?" It was midnight, so I knew it wasn't good.

"Someone's breaking into the Froeses' house. I'll take a dog and go over."

We both knew the Froeses' house was a picnic to enter. There were no iron bars over their doors or windows, no dog, no guard. Not that those were foolproof, as we could recently attest, but they at least slowed criminals down a little.

"Can you come lock the doors behind me?" Baseball bat in one hand and a can of newly acquired pepper spray in the other, he dashed down the stairs.

I pocketed my own can of pepper spray and didn't let Jarod more than six inches ahead of me.

"You sure we're okay out here?" I was trembling, even though the threat was at the Froeses'. I wondered if I'd feel this vulnerable in the dark the rest of my life.

"The dogs aren't barking at all, Jen. They'd let us know if someone was lurking." He closed the door between us. "I've got to go. Pray."

"I will." *What else could I possibly do?*

I locked the porch doors as quickly as I could, while Jarod called for Matye to open and close the gate. Then I made a mad dash up the stairs, locking the metal door behind me.

Sarah—now sleeping in our upstairs guest room—heard the commotion and opened her door, fear in her eyes. "What's going on?"

"The Froeses called—they're being robbed."

Her hand flew to her mouth.

"Jarod went to help." I was glad he was courageous enough to go, but afraid to be home without him. I sighed. "I don't think we're going to get any sleep till he's back home. Why don't we pray together."

We waited an hour till his tap on the horn brought our pulses back to normal. But his report was anything but calming: Dan, the Froese's visiting adult son had encountered the thieves as they bagged electronics on the first floor. They grabbed a kitchen knife, held it to his throat, and marched him upstairs. Knowing the rest of the family was locked behind a bedroom door, the thieves threatened to kill Dan unless they came out and cooperated. Thankfully, Tom was armed with pepper spray. He burst out of the door, spraying the thief in the eyes. The thieves evacuated. The Froese's lives had been spared, but the pepper spray in the air along with the very real threat they'd just endured made for a difficult night.

*God, could we all just feel secure now for a while?* I really didn't want any more drama.

"Now who is it?" This time I jumped up out of bed. "Jarod! Grab your phone!"

"Nooooo," Jarod moaned. "Not again."

We'd lost count, but this had to be around the fifth time Tom and Helen's home was broken into. If that's what it was. The Froeses were in Canada right now, but John was staying at their house.

"Jarod, who is it?"

He finally grabbed the phone. "John? Is that you?"

I could here John yelling on the other end of the line.

"Jarod, I need your help! These people are throwing rocks in the windows! I'm throwing the rocks right back while I tell them they need Jesus, but I need some help! Can you come?"

"I'm on my way, John." Jarod hung up, then smiled.

"Jarod, it's not funny!"

"He's evangelizing the thieves, Jen. Only John!" And out the door he went.

201

John was one of a kind. He was raised by a Bible-believing mama in Miami, but turned to gangs, drugs, and violence as a teen. In the aftermath of 9/11, John was part of the U.S.'s "clean sweep" and was deported back to Haiti, where he was welcomed with jail time. Upon his release, he remained unchanged. The only thing that could've lured him into church was a pretty girl. In fact, he found himself following one such girl down the aisle for an altar call. His "conversion" was unintentional and insincere, but once a neighbor saw what he'd done, she admonished him to read his Bible—*"That's what Christians do!"*

Reading Scripture in English, his first language, he finally understood the gospel, and that's when the changes began. His new passion was to share the gospel with a different person each day.

And on this day—or night—God brought the people right to his door.

Jarod came home with the oft-repeated tale; the thieves were gone by the time he had arrived. Tonight the SWAT team had also shown up, but for all their machine guns and padded bullet-proof vests, they were useless. They stood outside the gate, afraid to enter till Jarod led the way with his trademark baseball bat and pepper spray.

The whole routine was getting old. While we were all grateful to be alive, we were also growing stressed and weary. As months slipped by, the rash of break-ins finally slowed.

But an internal battle waged on.

I'd been through slumps before. Like anyone, I'd gone through short seasons of the blues. But this was heavier. Everything felt hopeless—too much fear, too much stress, too much work, too many demands, and not enough sleep.

I'd heard dozens of women say that children grow up before you know it, but I was fully aware that such things only happened one painful day at a time. Tomorrow would be just like today. I'd be exhausted, apprehensive, overworked, and underappreciated. Sure, I'd smile at a funny antic, I'd kiss my husband, I'd accomplish a thousand things on the never-ending to-do list; but I would die a little more inside.

For weeks, I prayed halfheartedly for a better attitude, but I grew bitter. Why didn't anyone else see me? Understand me? Help me? It sounded melodramatic, but I couldn't shake it—that fingernails-scratching-a-chalkboard feeling when I saw Sarah reading a book or Jarod posting a blog. *After all, who made dinner, Brendan in tow, night after night? Who was potty-training Dora? Who washed the dishes? Who hadn't sat through an entire meal, slept through an entire night, or enjoyed an entirely peaceful moment in months?*

Other than sighs and complaints, I didn't know how to express my despair. I was a "capable" person. I came from a family of strong people—strong women. My mom and grandma had endured much and had survived—no, thrived. I knew they'd cried, grieved, and wrestled with God. They were real. They didn't gloss over their faith. But there was something in *me* that wasn't sure if I could be real with them, or with others. My heart yearned to let someone know how badly I hurt; but something, maybe my pride, held me back.

As much as I wanted to blame those closest to me, I knew their lives weren't a piece of cake either. Jarod had been plunged so deep into school and ministry responsibilities, not to mention the challenges of personality differences within the mission, that he was struggling to maintain his own sanity. I simply couldn't ask more of him.

And Sarah was learning Creole while simultaneously teaching kindergarten in this brand new language. She had a little free time and she helped out where she could, but she needed a healthy balance in life as well. Why should I make my problems her problems?

It was summer now, which meant intensified heat, increased breakdowns of generators, inverters, and vehicles, and worst of all, it meant missionary friends on vacation. While Tom and Helen were gone, Jarod was placed in charge of the ministry. The increased responsibility did mean a little less help from him, but even worse was the knowledge that we were the only missionary couple that couldn't pack our family's bags and take a break. It was like attending summer school while all our classmates experienced the thrill of no homework, pool parties, and trips to Disney.

This was our fourth year in Haiti—a length of time in mission work typically marked by a yearlong furlough. I'd been through summers before; watched others fly off to the joys of family gatherings, air-conditioning, and ice cream. I thought I'd grown accustomed to it, but somehow this one was unbearable.

As the sun set behind the mountains each evening, my heart fluttered. *What if tonight is the night thieves come back for revenge?* Each time the dogs barked at a lizard or rat, I'd startle out of sleep with a pounding heart. When the sun rose and Brendan's cries coerced me out of bed, I felt no joy or motivation to live. Knowing my friends were being refreshed while I slaved on embittered me. Every time the kids bickered, spilled, cried, and demanded, I felt a flame of white-hot anger kindle in my core. Though I would've laid down my life for my children, I could also begin to understand why mothers would do unthinkable things to those they loved most. My fury seethed right below the boiling point, and I felt myself losing the last threads of control with every wail, demand, and tantrum. Not only did I hate my lot in life, I hated myself.

# 14

## Hope

He restores my soul.

Psalm 23:3

*I can't keep living like this. I'm being eaten alive, Lord!* I threw myself to the bed and sobbed. Resentment toward Jarod, each member of my household, and every missionary who ever enjoyed a family trip back to the States flowed like poison from my mind to my heart and through every cell of my body. I wanted to destroy something or someone—to exact revenge on Joseph for ruining our adoptions, to rebel against God for allowing all of this, to do something drastic enough to prove to everyone around me that I needed help.

My tears turned to silent cries: *I'm afraid I'll do something horrible, God! I'm terrified. I'm exhausted. I'm desperate! Don't you see? There's no way out!* But even as my adrenaline pumped, my mind jumped ahead of my tantrum: What good would it do? I was only heading deeper into the darkness, and I'd already spiraled so far into the abyss of self-pity that I didn't recognize myself. I knew the antidote to darkness was light. But apart from an adoption miracle—which I'd long ago given up on—how could anything change?

Utterly depleted, I reached for my One Year Bible. *Just this once, God, could you show me something I've never seen before?*

My hope rose just a little as I flipped pages to find the reading of the day, but my expectations were soon let down.

Psalm 23.

*That's it? How are verses about sheep and oil going to help me today, Lord?*

I read on, expecting nothing.

"The Lord is my shepherd; I shall not want."

I scoffed, and a few tears ran down my cheek.

"He makes me lie down in green pastures; He leads me beside still waters."

*Lie down? If only!*

"He restores my soul."

And here I stopped.

"He restores my soul."

I was living in a spiritual desert that rivaled the Sahara. Those four words may as well have been an invitation into the turquoise waters of Tahiti.

*Are you serious, God? You can do that?* This from a woman who'd been studying Scripture since childhood.

I drank in the words one more time: "He restores my soul."

And suddenly the truth became real, piercing through all my cynicism. I was placing impossible burdens on everyone around me. It was no wonder they failed to deliver. My husband, friends, and family were powerless to perform the duties of my Savior—my Shepherd. Life was disappointing. Circumstances were impossible. My loved ones let me down regularly. But I was never supposed to place my hope in them. I finally saw that.

*Okay, Jesus. Be my Shepherd. Please, restore my soul!* I turned a wet face up to the ceiling. *Help me! I am such a mess!*

I was still on my bed, in a hot, cluttered room, but I had been spiritually plunged into the still, clear waters of restoration. God was listening.

I devoured the following verses.

"He leads me in paths of righteousness for His name's sake." *Of course. He will help me—after all, His holy name is at stake.*

"Even though I walk through the valley of the shadow of death, I will fear no evil, for you are with me; your rod and your staff, they comfort me. You prepare a table before me in the presence of my enemies; you anoint my head with oil; my cup overflows."

Like never before, I knew what it was to fear evil, and oh how ready I was for His comfort. I also knew what it was to prepare a table; the process of making three meals a day from scratch, setting the table, cutting and cooling the kids' food, and dishing out seconds and thirds before I'd had my first bite had frustrated me regularly. The beauty of Jesus serving me so tenderly humbled me. He wanted to feed me. He wanted to anoint my wounds with oil. He offered to keep my cup so full, filling it after every sip, that it would overflow. I didn't have to run on empty; I didn't have to live with a dry cup.

"Surely goodness and mercy shall follow me all the days of my life; And I shall dwell in the house of the Lord forever."

I'd spent the past months convinced darkness and despair would follow me all the days of my life. But here was restoration for my soul.

There was a knock at the door. Someone needed me for something urgent, as always. Drying my face with tissues, I opened the door. The needs remained. Mommy was in demand. I was still stuck. Nothing had changed.

Yet everything had changed.

A few days later, I was ready to think practically. I simply could not manage my present workload on my own in a place where refrigeration, laundry, grocery shopping, and cooking required exponentially more work than in the States. Since Jarod and Sarah had their own loads to carry, I was going to have to hire help. It was ironic—none of my stateside peers were in a position to consider hiring a maid of any sort, and the very idea would have seemed like a laughable luxury to them, but I was dragging my feet. My last experience had soured the whole idea. I'd managed to navigate most of my life without making enemies, but I felt like I'd failed when I had to dismiss Mary. The truth was, I liked to be liked. I didn't enjoy bossing others around—even nicely. But then again, I did want things done my way. I didn't appreciate having my living room rearranged when it was mopped. I didn't like my nesting bowls to be stacked with the biggest bowl teetering on top of the smaller ones. And my pride was insulted when my home-cooked meals were either drowned in Tabasco sauce or rejected entirely. But God was calling me to let go of privacy, let go of control, and allow someone not only to watch us through a fishbowl, but also to jump into the fishbowl with us. Yes, the pH balance of the water would be thrown off a bit again, but it was time for me to risk accepting help once more.

Madam Henson and Leann were from our church, and came with Pastor Monestime's recommendations. I felt we must be starting off on the right foot if he was willing to send them our way. But just in case, Jarod and I decided to hire them on a trial basis. Leann was serious, but sweet and willing to smile. I assigned her the job of shadowing Jaden. With Dora in full potty-training mode and Brendan newly mobile, I couldn't keep up with Jaden's thirst, bathroom trips, and death-defying antics. I showed Leann Jaden's puzzles, his physical therapies to develop his crippled left hand, and some of his other favorite pastimes. She demonstrated the patience of Job. Her forbearance meant she was able to endure hours of endless repetition and boredom. That also meant she put up with way too much mischief. But she was a keeper.

Madam Henson, on the other hand, was a melancholy soul. I knew her burdens must be numerous, so I tried to adjust my expectations accordingly. She sighed. Her footsteps were heavy and slow. She needed to rest when her head ached. And she felt free to say, "No, I can't do that today," when I asked her to complete simple small tasks. And so thirty days after I hired her, I found myself speaking the dreaded words, "I'm so sorry, but I will not be rehiring you."

She cried.

When I later learned how desperate she was to provide for her family, I wanted to cry too.

I longed to ease the loads these women of Haiti carried. My heart hurt for each one. I prayed for them. I smiled at them. I wanted them to know I considered them sisters and equals. But I also failed them. Even as I did my best to listen, to understand, to share the grace God had given me, I failed. Maybe I was too focused on my own needs and rights and not concerned enough with their fight for survival. Or maybe God had lessons to teach all of us in the pain of disappointment. I begged God to redeem my messes; to bless and reward hearts that were seeking Him; to work in spite of me. And of course, He did. I was not their hope—He was. When Madam Henson chose a teachable spirit in the face of being let go, I was able to help her find another job.

Then a missionary friend recommended Madam Kendy to us. She was smart, cheerful, hard-working, and *fast* (i.e., a gift from heaven). I had never seen a Haitian in a hurry until Madam Kendy. On the Caribbean islands, especially this one, it's one o'clock until the clock strikes two; so tardiness is never an issue. Anything worth doing is worth doing slowly. Things that could be done today can also easily be put off till tomorrow. But Madam Kendy interpreted the concept of time through a different set of lenses. By some providential "error," the gene of haste had been slipped into her DNA. And was I ever grateful. Taking another risk had paid off.

"Jen! Guess what?" Jarod threw his keys onto the table and set down the packages he'd picked up from his airport mail run.

"No idea. What?" Guessing games never work with my "idea man." There is no telling what will come from his mouth next. It could be a ministry plan, a wild invention idea, or a theoretical speculation on where the Sears Tower might fall if pushed over. This time, though, he would earn my undivided attention.

"I was talking to the Children of the Promise missionaries, and they said their orphanage is getting adoptions approved for couples as young as thirty years old!"

My jaw dropped.

"Haitian Social Services is relaxing their so-called age-limit law."

"So, we only have to wait till your birthday?" I gasped.

"Right! March is just around the corner. We should call our lawyer and ask her if there are any papers to get in order ahead of time."

Hope nearly exploded my brain and my voice rose two octaves. "Do you know how awesome it would be to not have to wait another five years?"

Obviously he did. He grinned and threw his arms around me. "We just might get these kids adopted yet!"

Jarod made the call, and it was confirmed. Lawyer Val would line everything up. Our job was to hire a Haitian social worker to complete a new home study and obtain new fingerprint clearances through the U.S. Consulate. We had our work cut out for us—these things required multiple trips to Port-au-Prince. But upon their completion, she would indeed be able to resubmit our paperwork to IBESR.

Several months and a few thousand dollars later, Jarod's birthday marked the beginning of a new wait. *Please, Lord, please, please, please, let this be the year!* It was my daily prayer.

Two years had passed since Sarah moved to Haiti, and it was time to say goodbye. She'd learned a second language, taught kindergarten, navigated the open market on our weekly grocery shopping trips, won the hearts of my kids and the Kids Alive kids, declined a couple Haitian marriage proposals, and accepted one from the States. She was moving back to Kansas until her soon-to-be husband moved her to Missouri.

We missed Sarah, but didn't have too long to mope around her empty apartment. A newlywed missionary couple—husband from Venezuela, wife from the Dominican Republic—needed a home, and ours was a perfect fit. Our common language was Creole, so we frequently laughed our way through heavily accented, stilted, grammatically mangled conversations. Leomar and Maireny were wonderful. We couldn't have asked for better housemates.

With Sarah gone, I was forced to brave an area I had hitherto largely avoided: the clamorous, carnivorous open market. I'd asked Jarod to snag more expensive produce along the road for long enough. My day finally came.

After visiting the comparatively sterile storefront markets, I parked the car, grabbed my shopping bags, and dove in at Sarah's favorite corner. Helpers and vendors instantly swarmed.

"Let me carry your bags!"

"Buy my oranges!"

"*Blan!* Do you want eggs?"

"Are you Sarah's friend?"

The last inquiry came from a small wrinkled figure whom I recognized as Sarah's regular market companion.

"Wi, Madam. How are you?"

Having my full attention, she worked to gain my sympathy. "My head is hurting. My eyes . . . they have a problem." She rubbed them with a calloused hand.

"I'm sorry. Do you need to sit down?"

"No, no! I'll carry your purchases." She hoisted a large hand-made basket to her head. She wanted more than comfort—she wanted to secure a weekly job. I had to admire her spunk. I'd feel even worse about loading this little woman's basket with produce than I'd felt about riding stick-figure horses up Citadel mountain, but I couldn't bear to rob her of her dignity.

"Very well," I said, and she guided me to all of Sarah's usual vendors, where I fought for my own dignity. Being a people-pleaser at market is no easy task. I wished I could buy something from everyone and bolster each personal economy represented, but I had financial limits too. A half hour of mud, sweat, and animated negotiations was more than enough for me. I reassured my new little friend that I'd find her again next Wednesday and drove to the airport for my final errand—mail pickup.

I pulled the car alongside the runway, then opted to turn it around before walking to the plane. I backed into a restaurant driveway to complete my repositioning job, when the Blazer dropped with a sickening *clunk.*

"You've got to be kidding me, Jen." I was disgusted with myself. This was an all too familiar dilemma.

I stomped the accelerator. Nothing.

Groaning, I opened my door and walked around the car. Sure enough: one of my wheels was suspended above the ditch. No amount of revving, changing gears, or rocking the car was going to change matters. Head held high to conceal my humiliation, I approached the nearest respectable-looking man who happened to be talking to a couple other men.

"Excuse me, monsieur, would you be so kind as to take a look at my car?"

Naturally, a white woman asking for help in such ridiculous predicaments was quite entertaining. The men stepped forward, clucking and muttering at my foolishness. To their credit, they resisted the urge to mock me. I walked back and sat in the driver's seat, knowing from previous experience that it would take them a few minutes to work out their group dynamics. Each man would voice his opinion, vie for leadership, then try to seize control by taking the wheel.

"Madam," The winner said through the open window, "we have to lift the car, then drive it forward."

"Okay, you lift, I'll drive." My tone was beautifully authoritative. But before I knew it, I was out and he was in, barking orders from my seat.

"You guys better not do anything stupid," I muttered through clenched teeth, as if I had room to talk.

"Hey Jen! What's going on? You need some help?"

I spun my head around, more than a little relieved to see Brad, a missionary friend, approaching me.

"I think I'm getting help already, but do you mind sticking around for a minute?"

As we watched, the men lifted the Blazer from its pit. The men cheered, and I joined in the applause until I realized the Blazer was not only back on the road but also continuing on down the road.

"What do you think he's doing?" I asked Brad, scratching my head.

"Uh," he looked puzzled. "Maybe he's just testing it to see if it's working okay?"

We waited a few moments longer.

"I'm a little worried, Brad!"

"Yeah. I think he's taking your car."

Brad dashed after him. "Hey! Stop the car!"

I couldn't even imagine what I would tell Jarod. I was already wondering how I'd explain another ditch episode, let alone the complete lack of a vehicle. *Um, Honey, I kind of lost our car today. Yeah, this guy just drove off in it while Brad and I watched.*

Brad sprinted and waved his arms while I watched in disbelief. *I'm not sure that's going to be enough to persuade the guy to return, but at least he's trying.*

To my great relief, the car finally slowed and then turned around.

I was nearly speechless as Brad returned. "Was he really going to just drive off?"

"I don't know for sure," Brad sputtered. "But I kind of think he was."

Brad and his wife Monica were preparing to leave Haiti. On the heels of our many car problems (unrelated to my escapades), they decided to bless us with the gift of their four-wheeler. Words could not express how grateful we were. We were soon four-wheeling pros. And Jarod was soon brimming with ideas of how we should forget about cars and invest in additional four-wheelers. He talked of four-wheeler passenger trailers, four-wheeler wagons, and four-wheeler rain covers. I was not quite the fanatic he was, but even I couldn't deny how perfectly suited four-wheelers were to the roads of Haiti. I was a bit self-conscious at first about taking to the streets in my skirts and helmet, but when the occasion demanded it, I was grateful for some extra wheels.

While my own car-driving "skill set" centered on positioning our Blazer at alarming angles, Jarod's downtown specialty was locking the keys in the car. And when that happened, which was regularly, it was now Jen on the four-wheeler to the rescue. I normally felt quite gratified to be the rescuer, since I had too often been the damsel in distress. Some days, though, were worse than others.

One such day I'd already been to town and back, put away my groceries, showered, and fed five children when Jarod called for help. He'd made a special trip into town to get to the bank before closing time, but had locked his keys in the car. If I hurried, he might still make it. I assured him I'd come as quickly as possible.

I grabbed the four-wheeler key and tried to start it to no avail. I added gas and tried again. Nothing. After some priming, I was finally successful. I assured my whining children I'd be back soon and left them with Madam Kendy and Leann. I bounced my way to the bottom of our mountain road when it dawned on me that I'd left the extra set of car keys at home. So much for any righteous indignation about Jarod's absentmindedness.

Back up I went and through the routine: honk, gate, dogs, kids, chaos, keys, kids, dogs, gate, out.

I drove down again, not exactly enthusiastically.

*I was all clean. Now I'm going to get filthy again.* Splash. Prediction confirmed. Not only would I have to take another shower, I'd also have to change into a third outfit.

I arrived at the city gate. Bank-closing time a mere five minutes away, I veered off the main route onto a recently discovered shortcut, patting myself on the back for my clever move. Several yards onto the street though, I noticed I was the only "brilliant" driver fighting the flow of traffic. Somehow as I'd previously traversed this road, my cerebral computer had highlighted "shortcut" but failed to input "one way." As the taptaps honked, and passersby oh so helpfully pointed me in the right direction, I turned myself around (taking care not to fall in any ditches). Fuming at the inconvenience and ineptitude of my rescue mission, I waited at the intersection for a chance to rejoin the main thoroughfare. Nervous about a particularly sketchy vendor trying to sell me sunglasses, self-conscious about the annoyed taptap drivers behind me, and eager to speed my way to Jarod, I beeped my own tiny horn at the pedestrians crossing the street in front of me. *Just keep cool even though you feel vulnerable,* I chided myself. *Act confident, be dignified.* Just as my frustration at Jarod and every other soul blocking me from my destination peaked, I shifted my foot. By some unexplainable act of physics, and some act of a God, who did not mind taking my pride down another notch, my flip-flop sailed through the air, into a puddle of liquid filth.

*Beautiful.*

And so everyone in the world stood still and waited for me—frantic, humiliated me—as I climbed off the four-wheeler, reclaimed my sandal, and slid my foot into black slime. Everyone in the world, that is, *except* the bank employees.

# 15

## Open Doors

For the love of Christ controls us.

2 Corinthians 5:14

THANKSGIVING 2008

"Those guys are going to be hungry tomorrow, Jen. You'd better be making tons of food," Jarod said as he and Justin dripped sweat onto the kitchen floor. They'd just played a game of American football with a very unique group of guys—deportees, those who'd been deported from the United States back to Haiti. As we'd become better friends with John, he'd told us about the many others in his situation. These young men were viewed as the worst of the worst by the general Haitian population. They dressed like gangsters, were fluent in English, didn't speak Creole too well, and were assumed to have committed heinous crimes. Most of them had, in fact, belonged to gangs and been involved in unsavory activities, but many of them had been deported in the wake of 9/11 and weren't actually the hardened criminals they were made out to be. They weren't welcome in churches, and there were no missions reaching out to them in our area. Moved by John's burden for his friends, Jarod and I decided to organize a football game to break the ice, then host a Thanksgiving meal. They were elated.

"They told me they're taking *laxatives* tonight so they have plenty of room for tomorrow's meal," Jarod said.

"That," I said, grimacing, "is disgusting." I scrutinized the menu I'd scribbled out. "Now you've got me worried that I won't have enough." But after I reviewed my plans, I couldn't imagine needing more. I had a turkey, four chickens, stuffing, nine loaves of homemade french bread, mashed potatoes and gravy, sweet potatoes, corn, green beans, cranberry sauce, apple cake, and eight pies. If this failed to fill their recently emptied guts, that was their problem. But I hoped there'd be enough to feed my own family too.

"I should've made more," I told Jarod twenty-four hours later as we finished our meal. But I hadn't, and there simply had to be an end to the meal. A few guys begged to take the last few morsels of pie home to their girlfriends. After hiding one sliver away for myself, I obliged. As they piled into our SUV for their ride home, their boisterous banter gave way to words of appreciation.

"I can't remember the last time someone did something kind for me."

"This brought back such good memories."

"You guys are different from the other Christians down here."

My meager portion of the mouthwatering meal hadn't filled me up, but their humble gratitude satisfied my soul.

Jarod and I talked and prayed for the next few months about how to invest more deeply into these men's lives. Before long we found ourselves discipling the guys and their girlfriends—homemade ice cream in one hand, Bible in the other. The Holy Spirit began to work, and James and Magalie, unmarried parents of three, were back in church and ready to show obedience to Christ through marriage.

Not quite as thrilling as this act of commitment was Magalie's request that I be her *matron*—matron of honor. A sixth sense told me that this honor carried with it a huge amount of responsibility (and possibly financial obligation). But unable to form the word *no* in the face of such sweet and sincere appreciation, I capitulated. My accommodating nature soon earned me the privilege of helping fund the wedding gown rental, hosting flower girl dance practices, scouring the open market for little girls' tights, dresses, and shoes, opening my kitchen to Haitian "chefs," and utilizing my home as wedding-day launchpad/taxi service. Again, I floundered outside my comfort zone. *I don't have time for this. We're running out of money! What was I thinking?*

But in the mix was the joy of seeing Magalie realize her girlhood dream—a ceremony in which she was queen for a day, in which she donned the heavy white gown, beaming in the rightness of what was being done. She'd assumed she'd spend the rest of her life as James's woman—cooking his meals, raising their kids, never able to afford this luxury. But it was finally happening—her day of joy, and though Celine Dionne's "Because You Loved Me" would be stuck in my head for weeks, I was privileged to play a part.

Jarod's parents were coming for a late Christmas visit. As the kids and I set up our fake tree to the tunes of a Mannheim Steamroller Christmas album and wails of "Jaden, noooooo!" "Justin, I wanted to hang that ornament!" and "Brendan broke another one!" I let my mind go "there" again. *Could we possibly celebrate the next Christmas in the States?* My longing for us to be an official family with all the freedom that would bring intensified with every passing month. *I wouldn't mind coming back here, Lord,* I prayed. *I just want my kids to experience family togetherness . . . just taste the sweetness of a Thanksgiving or Christmas alongside grandparents, cousins, aunts, and uncles.* I wanted them to feel they belonged—I wanted to belong again. Like the Jewish toast "Next year in Jerusalem!" I clinked the lights and ornaments, silently toasting "Next year in the U.S.!" I couldn't help but remember the first Christmas I'd put up this very tree in our Chicago apartment—so hopeful our toddlers would soon join us.

That was forever ago. I took in the cacophony around me. So much had happened since then. Three more babies, ministry change, deliverance from danger, and yet, no adoptions. But this year there was hope, I reminded myself. We could receive word of an IBESR approval any day. Others' papers were coming through; surely ours would too. *Next Christmas in the U.S. . . . .*

Jarod's parents shipped boxes of gifts a couple weeks ahead of their flight, so they wouldn't be burdened by luggage. When I discerned that they'd given me the coffeemaker I'd requested (replacing the one I'd broken), I swore Jarod to secrecy and unwrapped it early. They wouldn't be in Haiti on the 25th; they wouldn't even know I'd opened it before Christmas.

Judgment clouded by coffee-brewing zeal, I failed to account for my tendency toward haste-induced clumsiness. I chipped the coffee pot rim *before* Christmas, a mere week before their arrival. There was no choice. In light of a previous laptop fatality, the death of a digital camera, and other minor offenses involving items they had purchased for us, I'd simply have to purchase another carafe before they saw my foolishness.

An online vendor sold redemption in the form of carafes for only ten dollars. *Perfect.* But then check-out: regular shipping cost another ten. *Yes, my pride was worth it.* But the estimated arrival date didn't look promising. *Priority shipping?* An additional twenty. I couldn't do it.

Regular shipping and lots of prayer it was. But God didn't buy into my urgency. Jarod's parents arrived, and I humbly served each morning's coffee from the chipped carafe. I weighed my options: Tell a silly, self-abasing story about how I managed to break their gift before it was even supposed to be opened, or hope their eyesight was bad enough to miss the glaring imperfection.

Surprising myself, I opted for the second. I was growing weary of dramatic apologies; I just wasn't sure I could pull off the same-song-seventieth-verse with humor.

To their credit, my gracious parents-in-law didn't say a word about it. I loved them for it.

The day after they left, I got my box. Making up for the delay,

God smiled on me: instead of only one carafe, there were two. He knew what I needed before I even asked Him; there was no denying I'd eventually put that second carafe to good use.

It was almost a year after Jarod's thirtieth birthday. Not a day passed that my heart didn't hope for *the* phone call from our lawyer. The miraculous news . . . the proof that God saw, God knew, God cared. We'd prodded a little—we didn't want her to somehow forget us—but understanding how slowly things move in the legal world of Haiti, we'd also been careful not to be a nuisance. She was a professional, and she was on our side. But with an entire year behind us, we finally checked in on her again.

The truth felt like déjà-vu: After creating a few papers for Daphne, Lawyer Val let our adoptions sit, now claiming that IBESR had lost our dossiers. Preoccupied with legal matters carrying heftier price tags, she just hadn't found the time to pursue our work, nor the courage to tell us she was too busy for us. And it left me in shock.

*Was this our ranking forever? Too far down the priority list to merit God's attention?* Theology told me otherwise: He sees the sparrow, He clothes the lilies—how much more does He care for us? But we'd been asking, seeking, and knocking for five years now. When was it enough? How much faith did He require? What was I missing?

The lines between human responsibility, spiritual warfare, and lessons in trust blurred. Like every human before and after me, I longed for clear directives, for solutions and answers. But God's concern was the same as always—the condition of my heart.

Would I trust the One who'd put our family together? The One who'd shone just enough light on the dark path for us to take the next step? Would I remember yesterday's protection, miracles, and provision?

Again I needed His arms around me when the "why" went unanswered. There was simply no logic here. No reasons—in my book—that were good enough. My faith was battered. I wasn't sure it could be any bigger than a mustard seed.

"Can we talk with Dixie?" I asked Jarod.

The two of us had managed to leave the kids in our housemates' care and get away for a short lunch together downtown. We talked over our burgers and Cokes, ocean breezes and restaurant ceiling fans drying the moisture from our foreheads.

"Let me see if I still have her phone number." He pulled out his cell phone while I polished off my remaining French fries.

Our year in Port-au-Prince had taught us how few adoption agencies could be trusted. But the one organization we'd seen run with integrity was God's Littlest Angels, founded and operated by Dixie and John Bickel. Dixie had completed adoptions throughout the difficult six years we'd been in Haiti, even for couples in their thirties.

"Yep, I've got it." Jarod wiped his mouth with a napkin. "If anyone can help us, it'll be Dixie."

I couldn't help but think it: *If only we'd gone to her years ago.*

Only days later, we traveled to Port to meet with her. We discussed logistics, found our "lost" dossiers in IBESR in a matter of minutes, then updated our papers over the course of the following week. As we handed the precious stack of documents into her keeping, she assured us there was no reason why our adoptions would not be approved. There could be hiccups, but nothing she and her lawyers hadn't already dealt with.

It was music to our ears.

I was done homeschooling. Between Jaden's special needs and Brendan and Dora's toddler demands, I couldn't have done it another day. For the first time, we had funds for the local Christian school. Cowman International blended the cultures of North Americans and English-speaking Haitians, both among the staff and in the student body. I was almost giddy anticipating my upcoming degree of freedom. But before relief . . . more pressure.

Our kids' birthmothers, Siliana and Veneste, hadn't visited in at least a year, but tonight they'd traveled together from Port and surprised us. They knocked on our gate, rousing us from sleep, famished and exhausted by their trip. But not merely from the journey, I soon learned—Siliana hadn't eaten in three days. Her bones protruded more than usual. Veneste wasn't much better off.

*What does one do for such brokenness?* I wondered, reeling from my own tiredness. There would be no waiting till morning, so I offered some bananas, rich in protein and potassium.

"At this time of night?" Siliana said. "That would kill me."

I'd never been as hungry as she, nor as steeped in the details of superstition that frequently dictated her menu choices.

Befuddled, I scrambled eggs and attempted to make our guests more comfortable.

Nothing in my relationship with my children's birth mothers was simple. I loved them; they overwhelmed me. When I'd had the opportunity to provide a job for one of them, it was soon abandoned. I probed their hearts—did they share my faith in Jesus? Their answers paralleled the average Haitian churchgoer, leaving me uncertain. I longed to bless them, serve them, give them myself and my resources; but their neediness quickly drained me. I was their children's mother. They would always have the bond and memories of those children in their womb, of infant eyes and infant cries.

Justin was old enough and perceptive enough to feel the tension. He saw Siliana's traits in his face, shared her dramatic tendencies, her love of the spotlight. His heart was tender to his half brother, Dora's age, and even the uncles, cousins, and grandparents that filled Siliana's stories. Yet he was undeniably ours, and somehow he saw that a life as Siliana's son wasn't possible. The tug-of-war would play out for years, a lifetime. How could it not?

All I could do was wade through the brokenness, the awkwardness, and the inner fatigue it all brought. All I could do was trust that somehow God could work all things for the good of those who love Him.

The night before their return to Port, I compiled supplies—anything they could eat, use, or sell—all they could carry. But in the wake of Hurricane Gustav, Hurricane Hanna descended in a fury. The flooding of Gonaives—the midway point on the only cross-country highway—meant the entire nation was stuck. Worse than stuck, the people of Gonaives were devastated—again. Stories of death filled radio airwaves: families drowning in their homes, adults and children alike sinking into waist-deep mud. Northern Haiti ran low on fuel—deliveries couldn't pass through Gonaives, so prices rose, lines for the last gallons of gas ran long, and hearts grew heavy.

While Gonaives fought the flood, I fought selfishness. Siliana and Veneste would be stuck in Cap Haitian until buses could again travel the only highway to the capital. Once more I felt the tension of life in a fourth-world country: choose self-pity for the inconvenience this created for me or think beyond myself and move a little further past my comfort zone. As usual I felt I had one foot in each camp.

I prayed for the grace to host them indefinitely, but all of us were relieved when an offer from my mom provided a solution. She sent funds to fly them back to Port. They happily took their leave and were united with their young sons in a matter of hours. And I returned to my slightly simpler existence, and to the feeling of smallness mixed with gratitude that can only come from catching a glimpse of the hardships of others.

The update from Dixie wasn't good. Our dossiers had been in such tiptop condition—our paperwork was deemed "simple" enough—that it had all been handed to "the less-experienced lawyer," and then there had been a fire, and some papers that had been destroyed had to be remade. It was always something. It was always *us*. We were forever the exception—the one family for whom something went wrong.

Then again, there was also always some new promise of possibility. As we shared our frustration in conversation with Pastor Monestime, his eyes lit up. "You know . . . there is a senator in Port-au-Prince—Senator Kelly—who is from Cap Haitian. He's still a member of our church. I wonder if he could help push your papers through IBESR."

"You would ask him for us?"

"Of course. I'll call him tomorrow."

When Pastor was finally able to reach him several days later, the senator agreed to help . . . as soon as his vacation was over. We spread the word to family and friends praying in earnest that Senator Kelly would fulfill his commitment. It could be so simple—just a quick phone call to the right person. Maybe this time it would work out. Maybe.

It was getting late. Well, late for us, but I was so enjoying setting up my new kitchen. Over the past week, I'd painted the walls red, and Jarod and our friend Matt had installed IKEA cabinets, shipped from the States. The kids were in bed now, allowing Jarod and me some extra time to tinker with towel and spice racks.

A lot had happened leading up to our home rearrangements. We'd temporarily housed a missionary couple downstairs. Then we'd hosted Sharon as she completed her Haitian daughter's adoption. Our friend John had taken up residence in our dependans when our guard Matye married. Now, in preparation for another missionary couple to move in downstairs, we created a kitchen for ourselves on the second story.

"It's almost ten o'clock," Jarod said. "How about I turn off the generator and then we go to bed?"

"Sounds good." Giving my new favorite room a final gaze of approval, I turned off the light.

Jarod pocketed a canister of pepper spray and grabbed the house keys, and I made my way to the bathroom for my evening shower.

As I winced in the icy water, a loud crack startled me. *What could have fallen?* I rinsed as quickly as possible and threw clothes back on to investigate. It sounded like corrugated tin slapping cement. But it had to be really heavy to have smacked so loudly.

I ran to a screened window with a view to the yard below. "Jarod?" I had to yell to be heard above the barking of the dogs.

The tone of his reply caught me off guard. It was tense and short. "Jen! Come down and lock the doors."

"What's going on?" But I didn't stay to hear his reply. I ran downstairs, and another crack broke the air.

"There's someone out here," I heard him yell. "Hurry!"

My stomach knotted, and as I locked the downstairs doors, I wondered how fear could create such instantaneous pain. I ran back upstairs—back to a window. This time around I would help. I'd use my adrenaline to fight instead of faint. "Can I throw a pepper spray grenade?" It was already in my hand.

"Not yet." This time Jarod's voice came from the back of the yard. He yelled for John to get his gun. *What gun?* I wondered. Seconds later, the two of them rushed to the darkened front yard, pepper spray canisters in hand. I stayed by the open window, ready—even eager—to throw my mace grenade. But in the few moments the guys had regrouped in the backyard, the attacker had escaped.

Jarod and John made their way upstairs, trying to sort through what had actually happened in such a fast-paced five minutes.

"I think he jumped the wall right after the second shot," Jarod was saying as they reached the kitchen.

"Shot?" I stared blankly. "Wait. That was a gun?"

"It was." Jarod tossed his keys and pepper spray onto the cabinet. "But I don't think he was using real bullets."

"What else would they be?"

"Blanks. There's no way he could have missed from that close."

"But he was shooting at you?" *How freaked out was I supposed to be?*

"Yeah. He'd shut the dogs into the garden area and was waiting close to the generator. As I walked toward him, he shined a flashlight at me with his right hand. I reached into my pocket for my pepper spray and he took a shot at me with his left hand."

"Maybe he thought your can of spray was a gun," John said.

"You're probably right," Jarod said. "It seemed to surprise him when I pulled it out. I was only a few yards away, but he missed. Maybe because he was using his left hand."

"Then what?" I asked.

"I ran backward toward John's room, and ducked behind the wall back there. But I remembered I'd left the door to the house open. I peeked out to make sure the guy wasn't headed into the house. He saw me stick my head out, and he shot again."

I shuddered. *How was Jarod not dead?*

John jumped in. "Then you told me to get my gun."

"Yeah," I interrupted. "What was that about?"

"I just wanted to use the Creole word for gun so it would scare the guy!"

"Well, I think it worked," John said. "I thought that's what you were probably doing."

"Thanks for joining me," Jarod said. "Once I knew Jen had locked the house door, I figured being aggressive was our best bet."

I still couldn't believe Jarod had just escaped two bullets. My stomach still hurt. And John looked a little shaky too. But Jarod didn't really seem fazed. I looked at him, puzzled. "Are you as okay as you seem, Hon?"

"Yeah, I'm fine. Plus, I still don't know if those were real bullets."

But the next morning confirmed they were. A policeman serving on an American mission team came over to take a look at our "crime scene." The shells of a .35 caliber revolver proved the danger had been greater than we realized but at the same time instilled in us an even greater awe of God's goodness. It was one thing to *say* we were completely secure when in the center of God's will, and another thing entirely to experience it. We were again on high alert each night, yet more aware than ever that our safety rested in the hands of an Almighty God. In fact, Jarod was less afraid than ever. "If God can protect me when I'm inches away from bullets, why should I bother being afraid anymore?"

He had a point.

Jarod rarely answered calls from unrecognized numbers, but something prompted him to answer this one. I watched his eyebrows lift in surprise as he listened to the caller.

"You'll never guess who that was," he said, hanging up.

I had nothing.

"Pastor Mark Riley."

"What? What did he say?"

"He's coming to Cap Haitian tomorrow to visit the radio station. He wants to know if we can meet him."

My heart fluttered a little. "So we're going to?"

"I think we should, don't you?"

There was so much history. Respect and love mixed with the sting of rejection and misunderstanding. But if he was reaching out to us. . . . "Yeah. I guess so." I sighed. "I wonder what he'll say."

"Me too."

The moment was upon us. I opened the car door and helped the kids get out of the back. They loved the grassy yard in front of the radio station headquarters, so they ran ahead of Jarod and me.

And there he was. But Mark didn't give us long to wonder what to do. He strode forward and offered open arms, which we accepted.

A few minutes into our small talk at a picnic table, Mark grew still and solemn.

"I want to tell you. . . . I'm sorry for so much." He looked down for a moment, then back into our eyes, back and forth between us so we'd see his sincerity. "I asked you to do things that I shouldn't have asked of you. I deeply regret that."

He leaned forward across the table. "Will you—can you—forgive me?"

We knew we would probably never see eye to eye on past issues. Probably not a whole lot in the future either, even if we tried. But we knew this was the time to set down stones. His apology validated the deep concerns that had led us away.

Jarod spoke first. "We forgave you a long time ago, Mark. Thank you for your apology. And we weren't blameless either, so please accept our apologies as well."

Mark nodded, then looked to me.

"Of course we forgive you," I added, blinking tears. "This means a lot."

As we said our goodbyes, Mark asked about our adoptions.

"We've handed them over to Dixie Bickel, plus we're hoping for help from a senator," Jarod said. "We could receive word of IBESR approval soon." Memories of Joseph's corruption, which had hindered us from the very start, pulled and taunted. But this was a day of forgiveness. There was no use holding on to that bitterness.

But Dixie's next update wasn't encouraging: "Your papers have been sent to President Preval's office. The fact that you have your own biological children is causing a new problem. He's been granting special approvals for others in your situation, but of course, it will take a bit more time."

That certainly wasn't shocking. It was the story of our lives.

# 16

## Standing on the Promises

My grace is sufficient for you,
for my power is made perfect in weakness.

2 Corinthians 12:9

"We've done it again." I didn't even want to say it. "Our keys are right there—locked in our car."

And this time was worse than usual. Our whole family was in Fort Liberty, an hour away from home. Our spare car key was in our house, and our house key was, of course, in our Land Cruiser.

A few young men saw us trying to pry our windows open and stopped to ask if we needed help. They spoke in English, but I answered in Creole, not sure if they'd really understand.

"No, mèsi." My resourceful husband would figure something out.

"My uncle lives close. I can find something to open the window," one of them said. I protested, but he sprinted off anyway. Jarod and I were discussing which window we should break when the young man jogged back with a flat iron bar. We decided to humor him for a few minutes before taking a rock to a window. To our amazement, he soon pushed a back window open. Relieved and grateful, we spent a little extra time talking with him. His English was heavily accented, but fairly extensive.

He introduced himself as Wilkenson and told us he was from Fort Liberty, but actually lived in Cap Haitian at a boys' home. He looked to be in his late teens, but told us he was already twenty and had been part of the home since he had been given up by his parents several years earlier. As we said goodbye, we invited him to visit our church that weekend.

Wilkenson not only showed up but also went forward for the invitation at the end of the service. When we spoke to him afterward, he told us he'd accepted Christ years earlier, but was now fully committing himself to the Lord. We deepened our acquaintance over Sunday dinner at our house, and let him know we'd stay in touch.

A few weeks later, his orphanage was closed. The American priest who'd previously managed the home was convicted of abuse. The scandal shut down funding, and dozens of boys were suddenly homeless. A dejected Wilkenson, who himself had been abused, went back to live with relatives in Fort Liberty—relatives deeply entrenched in voodoo.

There'd been no word from Wilkenson for a few weeks when he showed up at our door. Even as I greeted him, it was clear he wasn't well.

"Come in, Wilkenson." I walked alongside him from the gate to the porch.

His speech was halted, his eyes glazed. "My family . . . they want me to do voodoo. I said no. Then they burned me with cigarettes." He held out his arm as proof, then pointed to burns on his face and neck. "I don't know where to go. They will persecute me. I'm suffering so much. *Map soufwi anpil.*"

"Please, sit down. I'll bring you some water." I pointed to a plastic chair on the porch, then flew upstairs in search of Jarod. *God, what do we do?* Would I never cease to be overwhelmed? *What are we dealing with here? Is this shock? PTSD? How do we handle this? What are we called to do?*

Finding Jarod at his computer, I breathlessly brought him up to speed, finishing with, "Do you think we should let him stay here?"

We rejoined Wilkenson on the front porch to try and learn more. By the end of our conversation, we agreed we should offer him a room in the dependans. And in so doing, we took on a set of needs deeper than any we'd known so far.

We had to deal with the basics, of course: school, uniforms, and daily transportation to school were paid for through an American sponsor. I made and served the meals. But it was the listening, the caring, and the praying that meant and cost the most. Maybe if I'd known how much this feeling and sharing of his burdens would drain me, I'd have turned him away. I felt the heaviness of his abuse from years past in the orphanage. I shared just a portion of his trauma as I heard more stories of mistreatment because of his faith. And each night as my head hit my pillow, I wondered what story of spiritual battle I'd hear from Wilkenson in the morning. The demonic forces seemed intent on winning Wilkenson back to their side, relenting only after fervent prayer spoken in Jesus' name.

For a season, Wilkenson healed and thrived. But this was followed by a series of absences from school, which he explained only by "headaches."

How were thirty-somethings supposed to parent a twenty-something? From another culture? With a history of abuse? Who remained enigmatic despite our best efforts to know and understand? I had no idea. Once more, my heart was broken, and I was in over my head.

The caller ID on my phone showed Dixie's number, and my hopes soared. Despite nothing but letdowns over the past seven years, despite a sneaking suspicion that God was using the adoption delays to keep us in Haiti when we might have been tempted to run away, on the good days, I could still imagine that *someday* the news would be good. *Lord, could it just please be today?*

"Hello?"

"Jennifer, your papers came back from the president's office. . . ." My pulse throbbed.

"But they weren't approved. They say the president won't sign your dossier because you are both under the age of thirty-five."

We were crushed. But there was simply nothing left to be done. We had waited seven years already; what was another two? Of course, it was another two years until Jarod was thirty-five and we could get this *first* step of the process completed. Who knew how many years it would be until the process was actually completed in full?

It really was staggering. Our independent lawyer had failed, Senator Kelly apparently couldn't have cared less, and now even Dixie was helpless.

It seemed unfathomable to be thwarted at every turn like this. How was it that hundreds of other families could adopt from Haiti each year, and we—living *in* Haiti, fluent in Creole, and on the "inside track"—would find it completely impossible to make it over the first hurdle in the course of seven years? Sure, many others encountered roadblocks in their adoptions; but there was a big difference between a one-year delay and a seven-year delay. It was practically a "miracle" that our adoptions *couldn't* get approved. What were the chances that one family could be rejected so many times? As Jarod and I took it all in, we began to believe God's plan might be far different than we'd ever imagined.

Maybe we would just apply for student visas when our children turned eighteen. Maybe the adoptions would never actually happen. We had no idea. All we knew was that our sovereign God was for some reason not answering our prayers the way we wished He would.

*Trust.*

The message never seemed to change.

And so we just lived. We had no more dreams of miraculous phone calls. There was just the here and now. The everyday trials. The everyday blessings. The everyday stress and the everyday mercies.

And then a diversion: scuba diving. When Nick Hobgood, an American USAID associate and certified scuba instructor, offered free lessons, his family and ours began traversing Haiti's untouched beaches together. Saturdays often found us riding bumpy roads or rickety boats to turquoise waters that should have been flooded with tourists. But the only beach foreigners go to is Labadee—accessible only by Royal Caribbean cruise ships.

The dives challenged me. I'm no daredevil, but I was competitive and intrigued enough to push myself a little. Nick was a thorough teacher. He allowed us plenty of practice in the water, but also made sure we understood the scientific details of diving. We studied dangerous sea creatures, charts, the specifics of water pressure, nitrogen levels, and decompression. We developed a healthy respect for the sport, understanding that careless mistakes made in Haiti could not be easily undone by decompression chambers or state-of-the-art medical care. Nick also emphasized that if we were particularly stressed, we should pass on that day's dive.

By now, stress was so normal I no longer recognized it. One normally stressful day, I dove into the waters of what the Hobgoods called Lemon Beach, and followed Nick to the bottom of the relatively shallow area. The water was a little hazy, but I could still see plenty of colorful sea creatures. The otherworldliness fascinated me, as always. It was hard to believe I was really doing this. I was pretty proud of myself, to be honest. A few weeks back, I'd passed an unpleasant test—sitting on the ocean floor, taking my goggles off with eyes open, then putting them back on, exhaling through my nose to blow the water out of them. I'd wondered ahead of time if I would panic, but I'd surprised myself by calmly completing the task with little trouble.

Today at Lemon Beach though, an odd feeling began to creep up on me: a feeling of such surreality that I felt I was completely detached from myself. I breathed slowly, in and out, through my breathing apparatus, trying remain calm. Had I been above water, I'd have snapped myself out of it through conversation, but in the eerie quiet below the surface, I was alone with my strange new sensations.

Nick pointed out several lionfish. It was the first time I'd seen the deadly, beautiful creatures in real life. I was thrilled to finally come upon them, knowing I was at a safe distance to admire then without fearing them. But even as I marveled, my heart pounded a little faster, and I began to feel increasingly unsettled. Finally, I approached Nick and gave him the thumbs-up sign, which in diving language signals a need to rise and surface. He flashed the "okay" signal, and we carefully ascended. Once on top the waves, I shook off my uneasiness, took some deep breaths, and then dove back down.

Back onshore, I confessed my discomfort. Nick assured me that the haziness of the water could have that affect on any new diver. I was encouraged, but as our families boated back home, I felt something just wasn't quite right.

Several weeks later, we celebrated the first day of 2010 with a dive off the shore of Fort Liberty. Nick had discovered a steep underwater cliff laden with bright corals, sponges, seaweed, and tropical fish. It would be our first group dive: so far, Nick had tutored us one on one, but now that we were becoming more advanced, he was confident the three of us could dive together.

We swam a couple hundred yards into the little bay before we began our descent. Careful to equalize our ears every few feet, we sank lower and lower into the blue. To our right was a wall of beauty—yellow, blue, and purple fish, orange corals, and delicate sea crabs. Above, below, and in every other direction was the deep blue of the sea. Had I been watching our dive in an Imax theater, my stomach might have quivered, yet I would have leaned forward in awe. But as I saw Nick and my husband eagerly push forward and downward, I realized my brain was not going to cooperate. The strange feeling of detachment, uneasiness, and mild panic pressed down on me. I did my best to push it away—to focus on the breathtaking beauty all around me, to avoid being the wimpy one in the trio, but it was no use. I kicked urgently ahead and tapped Jarod. I held my thumb up, feeling like a fool, yet desperate to rise to the land I knew.

Once we surfaced, I apologized for messing up the dive. Jarod assured me I would be fine—he knew I could handle the dive. I appreciated his vote of confidence, but knew my nerves were not in any state to take greater risks today. Doing my best to appear in control, I assured the guys that I could swim back to shore and they should finish the dive on their own.

As they dove back in, I shuddered. There was no way I would ever go back in. I loved the underwater sights, but needed to see it on a TV screen from then on. My head was spinning, my heart pounding, and I felt like a stranger to my own body. I couldn't collapse yet though. First I had to swim to the beach.

It wasn't as easy swimming back against the current as it had been coming in. Thankful that my wetsuit was buoyant, I fought the waves. In an attempt to keep calm, I turned onto my back and attempted to paddle myself in. A measure of panic induced an extra kick of adrenaline, which gave me the strength I needed to finally make it ashore. I sat on the beach, thanked God for empowering my swim, and lectured myself on my pride. *From now on, you just be honest, and admit it when you can't do something. You do not have to keep diving, no matter who else is! It's not worth this kind of stress!* I really hoped I would listen to myself.

Back at home that afternoon with kids settled down for naps, I sank onto my bed to relax. When my phone rang a moment later, the caller ID revealed a call from the States. Within seconds I was deep in conversation with my mom and grandma.

After the traditional Happy New Year greetings, my grandma told me she was suffering from a broken eardrum, a condition I'd just studied through diving instruction. I told her what I'd learned and about a friend who was recovering from the same ailment. As I assured her that it would heal and return to normal in a number of weeks, she commented on the irony of making a call all the way to Haiti to receive reassurance and medical advice when she was the one who lived in the land of experts and comfort.

Suddenly I was listening in slow motion . . . through a dark tunnel . . . words distorted and drawn out. "All . . . the waaaaay . . . out there . . . in Haiti."

I felt myself on the other side of the world from everything familiar, everything comforting and normal. I was in the deep blue of the ocean again—trapped in a bizarre and unfamiliar land where I could not breathe. Haiti closed in on me. In a flash I felt afresh the prison that held me—the adoptions, heat, corruption, isolation, and deep blue oceans swirled around me, and I broke into a sweat.

I breathed out a weak goodbye. I didn't want Grandma or Mom to know what was going on.

"I'm so glad I called you," Grandma said. "I feel much more encouraged about my ear."

I hung up, fanning myself, and leaned my head against my headboard.

*What was this?* I was safe! I was out of the ocean. The dive was over. I'd never dive again. *Get over it, Jen. You're fine.* I forced myself to my feet and walked to my bathroom, where I splashed cold water on my face.

*Lord, please. I don't know what this is. Please make it stop!*

But my heart pounded and throbbed, my knees shook, and worst of all, my soul was suddenly filled with dread and fear. I'd been scared before—terrified of the thieves that broke in, worried almost sick that they'd return . . . but those fears had objects. What was I afraid of now?

Never eager to admit weakness, I put off telling Jarod about my panic attack until that night in bed. In the darkness, which seemed infinitely more foreboding tonight, I asked in a whisper if he would pray for me.

"I don't know if it's just my dive that scared me, or if this is some kind of spiritual attack. I just know it's awful."

He hugged me close and offered a simple prayer. I lay there, fighting the heaviness with all the spiritual weapons I possessed—Scripture passages, prayer, thanksgiving. Finally I drifted off to sleep.

Any hopes that my episode of panic was to remain a one-time, random incident quickly faded. It was not a passing thunderstorm; it was rainy season. Though there was no tangible threat, I was convinced that doom awaited me around each corner. My heart simply would not listen to reason.

The thought of being alone was terrifying. I'd normally made trips into town on my own without a second thought, but now I begged Jarod to shop and run errands for me. I also carefully avoided driving anywhere. I just didn't know what would happen if panic hit while I was at the wheel.

A few days into January, we met up with some fellow Moody grads at the local cheeseburger joint. I felt decent. I was able to fake a normal, cheerful demeanor, push away the odd sense that I was listening to the voice of a stranger each time I heard myself talk, and just enjoy hearing their news. But when Jarod ran an errand after lunch, leaving the kids and me in the car, I grew agitated. His two-minute errand had taken at least ten, and now Brendan had to go to the bathroom.

Unable to wait any longer, I took Brendan out and stepped into the store Jarod had entered.

"He left a long time ago, ma'am," the clerk said.

I exited and looked up and down the street for my husband. *Don't panic. Don't panic.*

"Let's check at this store." I pulled Brendan by the hand, irrational fear gripping me as we stepped across the garbage-laden street. I struggled for breath. *Where are you, Jarod?* I may as well have been on Mars. The street that was so familiar overwhelmed me with its foreignness. I listened in confusion to my own voice speaking the Creole language, asking another store clerk if he'd seen my husband, then nearly collapsed with relief when I glimpsed Jarod in the back.

I worked to understand—to define what was happening. Knowing was supposed to be half the battle after all. Was this exhaustion? Surely I'd been more exhausted before. Was it about the dive? If so, why wouldn't the fear leave upon my vow never to dive again? Was I under spiritual attack? Maybe. I knew what weapons to use for that, at least. Was the stress of Wilkenson's issues affecting me? If so, then I felt worse for him than ever!

A new thought presented itself: the one-year anniversary of Jarod's assault was around the corner. I'd heard that people can react with panic and post-traumatic stress on anniversaries of traumatic events. I hadn't actually been thinking about it, nor did the memory of it stir any new fear or terror, but maybe the effects were subconscious.

Or maybe I was just having a mental breakdown. I was going crazy. That was the worst possibility of them all.

It seemed I was able to keep my composure outwardly as my insides churned. I spent the next week completing normal tasks—making meals, tending to the many needs of the kids, and doing housework. I spent all my free moments devouring God's Word and other sources of encouragement—hymn lyrics, books, and emails. I especially treasured email messages from my friend

Jamie, whom I'd confided in. She too had experienced panic and lived to tell about it. She, a few other friends, and my mom, whom I'd finally told as well, promised to pray fervently.

My battle was one of the mind. The underwater cliff of Fort Liberty became my reality; I was surrounded by deep, dark blue—enough to overwhelm and defeat me. Only this time, swimming ashore was not an option. There would be no escape, no chickening out of the test. I had been provided with the appropriate gear; the Spirit of God would be my breathing apparatus. This wasn't a test to the death—it only felt like it. But it was a test of my focus. I could look at the treasure cove on the one side—mining the truth and beauty of God's Word—or I could feed my fear with the endless blue on every other side.

> When darkness veils His lovely face,
> I rest on His unchanging grace;
> In every high and stormy gale,
> My anchor holds within the veil.
>
> His oath, His covenant, His blood
> Support me in the whelming flood;
> When all around my soul gives way,
> He then is all my hope and stay.
>
> On Christ the Solid Rock I stand
> All other ground is sinking sand,
>
> All other ground is sinking sand.

But so much more was soon to give way. Soon all of Haiti would be sinking sand.

# 17

## The Moving of Mountains

Therefore we will not fear though the earth gives way,
though the mountains be moved into the heart of the sea.

Psalm 46:2

JANUARY 12, 2010

It was close to five in the evening. I scanned my kitchen cupboards in search of a quick dinner. Having a task to focus on helped me fight panic.

But then the bottom dropped out. The white tiles shook beneath my feet. Dishes rattled. And while my world trembled, thousands of souls were buried forever in Port-au-Prince. At 4:53 p.m., the 7.0 magnitude earthquake escorted masses of Haitians into eternity.

I blinked in confusion one hundred miles away, still unknowing. The kids were roughhousing, and Jarod had just walked across our flat roof. *Had they somehow . . . ?* But no, I found Jarod outside, and as the earth stilled, he looked at me.

"That had to be really bad somewhere else."

The nation couldn't have been less prepared. Building safety codes were a joke. Everything crumbled. The National Palace, the Catholic Cathedral, hotels, banks, businesses, homes. Other countries had weathered worse on the Richter scale, but Haiti's corruption was exposed and paid for in lives. Every cement mixer who skimped, every builder who cut corners, every inspector who took bribes saw the fruit of their hands crumble. Reaping what had been sown was bitter, as bitter as the cement dust choking the city.

I'd never lived the true Haitian life on a normal day. But I'd seen it. And there were simply no words. Nothing adequate enough to protest the hopelessness of it all. Why those whose endurance had stretched beyond anything my American mind could conceive had to be pushed even further was past comprehension. Had the casualties been limited to the corrupt—those who'd withheld justice in the "Palace of Justice," the *chemiere* who'd terrorized the downtrodden, I would have read this as judgment. And even some Haitian churches proclaimed this an act of God's fist. But while death and devastation was a clarion call to repentance, it was also a reminder that it was only by the Lord's mercies that we weren't all consumed.

Aftershocks rocked the capital daily. Residents eventually learned to run outside instead of seeking refuge inside. That lack of knowledge alone accounted for countless deaths upon the initial hit. Statistics flooded in, changing by the hour. Thousands . . . tens of thousands, no, maybe hundreds of thousands were dead. Bodies covered the ground, and dust choked those still living.

Cries of those trapped inside houses and hotels filled the air, eventually giving way to ominous silence.

As Haiti reeled, the rest of the world took action. International rescue teams flew in to dig out the buried. The airport was closed except for relief efforts. U.N. troops, the U.S. military, and streams of doctors and nurses flooded the city. Again—and like never before—Haiti was at the mercy of its neighbors' compassion.

We found ourselves in an odd position. Our families in the States knew more than we did, thanks to nonstop news coverage. Our phones had limited connection to anyone in Port, due to downed cell phone towers. Furthermore, sketchy Internet access due to pouring rain kept us from in-depth online information. We wanted to help, but had to discern the best way to proceed. Teams from the States were already on the ground in Port, and here we were, only a hundred miles away, in limbo. But we had our own situations to consider—supplies from Port were now cut off and banks were closed. Money, gas, and food would soon be in high demand.

Jarod purchased one hundred gallons of fuel. He stocked up on groceries for the family, also making sure our children's homes were prepared. Our personal cash problem was solved by a visit from our Dominican Kids Alive supervisor, who transported funds from the Dominican Republic.

But once Jarod was sure our family's and ministry's needs would be met, he was ready to take action. Two days following the quake, he and Matt McCormick, a friend from Moody, also now in full time Haitian ministry, discussed possible plans. While rushing off to Port-au-Prince felt like the most natural response, their conversation unveiled a better idea. After assessing the needs of missionaries already in the trenches of Port, they could provide a supply line from the Dominican Republic. They emailed and called as many Port-au-Prince missions as possible and came away with a clear answer: Everyone needed fuel for generators—the source of light and power for endless operations—as well as formula for orphanages, food, water, and basic medical supplies.

Matt would soon escort his wife Pam and their kids back to Florida for the birth of their third child, but prior to leaving he networked with the U.N. troops of Fort Liberty to secure buses to transport supplies. He also recruited Moody grads Michael and Erika Philip in Florida to receive donations, making the purchase of the supplies possible. In the meantime, Jarod took orders from missionaries and clinics.

Saturday evening, the Hubele family, missionaries from down the road, braved the tropical storms and joined us for dinner. Our conversation rarely varied from the topic of the recent tragedy, but Rachelle was quick to inquire about our adoptions. "Do you think there's any chance they'd be expedited now?"

I shook my head. I'd already pondered it. The truth was, with the government buildings destroyed and all systems in an unheard-of state of chaos, there was now less hope than ever. Our adoptions may as well have been buried under the National Palace.

"I did look it up online," I told her. "And the U.S. is waiving the last step of the process. Typically, adoptive parents have to get a U.S. visa and passport from the Embassy. But if parents have completed the Haitian side of the process, the U.S. is making provision for them to skip those steps."

"So that doesn't help you?" Her eyes were still filled with hope.

I hated to disappoint her. "Not at all. We haven't even completed the first step of the Haitian process."

I sat in the kitchen, head in my hands. The "encouraging" article Erika Philip had just forwarded to me had me in knots again. "U.S. to Expedite Haitian Adoptions." It only reiterated what I'd told Rachelle the night before—the focus was on earthquake victims, namely those at the end of the adoption process. Adoptive American parents were in a panic. Requests flooded government offices: *"Help us bring our babies home!"* It made complete sense. Orphanages had crumbled. Supplies were low. New orphans needed help. Obviously, anything Haiti or the United States could do to bring chosen children home needed to be done. These were the children and parents in dire straits, not us.

I was ashamed of myself and my welling envy. The earthquake wasn't about us. We were alive. Safe. Fine. But it meant the death of our adoptions. Hot tears filled my eyes. How many times had I already been here, praying, hoping, asking, knocking, seeking? Watching everyone else get their heart's desire, while we stayed, we endured, we waited. *It's just not fair, God. It just doesn't seem fair.* My sobs were silent, but my internal cries were deafening.

*I know you see us. I know you do. I know you do. . . .*

I looked back up at the blurred screen and brought my fingers to the keyboard.

"Dear Erika, Thanks so much for the article. Unfortunately, we won't fit into this category. . . ."

We didn't fit into any category.

My phone rang in the middle of the night. I didn't know the caller, but answered anyway.

"Don't you remember me?" the woman asked. "I'm Magalie's mother. We met at her wedding."

She and I must have exchanged phone numbers at some point. I wasn't sure why she'd called me, but her sorrow came pouring out. She'd watched children and grandchildren die. She'd grabbed her eight-year-old granddaughter, doing all she could to shield her from the falling cement blocks. Yet she'd been hit. The child died on her lap.

"And now?" I asked. "Are you still in danger?"

"We're cut off from help and from supplies. Hunger is killing us now."

The torrential downpours continued.

The next day when Jarod came back from a trip to town, four passengers hopped out of the back of our muddy truck—Magalie and her three children. They each wore backpacks, and my instincts told me they'd be staying a while.

Jarod anticipated my questions as I greeted Magalie. "They were on their way to our house, so I gave them a ride. Their home is flooded."

"Oh I'm so sorry!" I ushered them inside, where her kids joined mine. "Where is James?"

"He's keeping an eye on the house," Magalie said. "Whenever it floods, people loot the empty homes. But he wanted us to find a better place to spend the day. So we thought we'd come visit you."

I smiled, knowing that "the day" meant more than the day.

It was hard for these families. James and Magalie were lucky in a sense—they actually owned a home. But the most affordable homes were down by the river. That meant they dealt with flooding every single rainy season. They risked losing everything by living there, but it was a chance they had to take.

We spoke of Magalie's mother. She said James would travel to Port for her mom as soon as he could get away. It's what everyone was doing these days—taking a bus to Port to look for lost relatives. And everyone had a relative in Port. That was where everyone went for education and jobs. Leann had just told me how hearing her phone ring filled her with dread: She knew it would only be news of yet another relative who had died in the disaster.

No one was untouched. The entire nation wept.

After a three-day stay, Magalie and her kids returned to their home. On Monday morning, I dropped Jarod off at One Mission Society (OMS) on my way to take the kids to school. He'd catch a ride to the Dominican Republic and oversee the purchase of the first supply shipment.

"I may be back tomorrow. For sure in a few days," he said as we said a hurried goodbye. I hated the idea of being alone. With my panic attacks and now all the turmoil, I dreaded his absence. But there was no way I wanted to hold him back from helping.

"I'll be praying for you," I called as he shut the door. I wouldn't see him for an entire month.

# 18

## Praying for Miracles

Be still, and know that I am God.

Psalm 46:10

I breathed a prayer of thanks as I walked back into the house with Brendan and Jaden. I hadn't been driving since my panic attacks began, so I was grateful I'd managed it this morning.

The boys soon busied themselves with toys, and I sat on the couch, eyeing my phone, deep in thought. *Dare I call Dixie?* I knew she would have called us if anything had changed—if there was any hope. But I decided I'd rather know the worst than be tortured, wondering. I hated to bother her. I knew she was managing her orphanage amid devastation, but I just had to know. *The phone probably won't work anyway. What's the harm in trying?*

It rang a few times. And then she answered. Talking with her always felt like my fate hung in the balance. I was always breathless.

"Do you have any idea what we should expect? I mean, I'm assuming the worst. I'm guessing we're back at ground zero now, right?"

"Jennifer, if you want to get your kids to the U.S., this might be your only chance."

I didn't know what to say, except to ask for clarification.

"I'm going to the Embassy on Wednesday morning. I'll make an appeal for visas for all my kids. All eighty-three, including yours. You need to pray."

I knew she was busy, so I tried not to hold her up for long, even though my questions multiplied by the second. As she said goodbye though, she warned that any departure for the States would be hasty. If her orphanage was to be evacuated, if visas were granted, a plane—maybe a military plane—would transport everyone at short notice.

It was almost too much for me. To be handed hope once more when I had steeled myself for endless worst-case scenarios was actually a burden. I wasn't sure I wanted it. Two days stretched before me—days without Jarod to steady me, days with five kids, daily struggles, and now a desperate, last-chance hope. But I had to take it.

I ran to the kitchen, where the laptop sat. Time to gather prayer support.

"Dear friends, there is a *chance*. . . ."

By now, Jarod, Matt, and Erika and Michael Philip had the cogs in place for their relief supply train to begin operating. I spent the rest of the day on the computer and phone, fielding supply requests from missions and clinics and relaying them to

Jarod. I was grateful for an outlet for my restless energy and thankful I could help in a small way.

The following day, one of Dixie's assistants emailed, asking me to provide up-to-date passport photos of our kids, just in case. I was careful not to raise the kids' hopes; they knew we were praying for the adoptions, but didn't know how high the stakes were. As was always the case in Haiti, a simple project turned into a many-hour ordeal. But by day's end we produced the photos.

As darkness fell and the stresses hovered over me, I wanted my little ones close. Dora and Brendan were small enough to fit into the bed with me, and I placed mattresses and blankets on the floor around us for Justin, Jaden, and Daphne. We prayed together: Prayed for the hurting in Port-au-Prince, prayed for Daddy, now in the Dominican Republic, prayed for our children's adoptions, and prayed for protection as we slept. Fans surrounded us, as always, wicking the sweat off our faces. Brendan and Dora, oblivious to the heat, attempted to snuggle close to me. My eyes were heavy and I longed for rest, but before I yielded to my exhaustion, I pleaded for grace. Tomorrow's news could change everything. I knew I'd need every ounce of strength God could give me.

The next thing I knew, the bed was vibrating. I forced my eyes open to the early-morning light and heat and saw Daphne's foot on the bed frame. "Daph," I said, keeping my voice low so as not to wake the others, "Stop shaking the bed."

"I'm not, Mom!" And she wasn't. It must have been another aftershock.

I let my head fall back again, and butterflies filled my stomach.

This was the day. Dixie had been sure she'd know something by the end of it.

*What do I today, Lord?* I asked. The possibilities filled my mind. We could continue as normal: school, chores, emails, meals. Keep the atmosphere calm. Or . . . Should I dare fill the kids in? Raise their hopes? Pack up for a walk across the Red Sea?

As my bed continued shaking, I closed my eyes. It was unsettling, but I was too focused on other things to panic. Again, I asked, *What do I do?*

There was no voice. No promise. But the seed of faith, that little grain of hope, seemed to gasp in a breath. *What if the news was good?*

I let my mind follow hope's trail. If we received word the visas were approved, we'd need to traverse one hundred miles today. If we had to leave, we'd need to pack, find a ride, close up the house, make provisions for Wilkenson. . . . The list was long.

*Pack.*

It was the riskiest but most logical thing to do. And with that word on my heart, I sat up. My adrenaline pumped as I made mental lists. Jarod and I had plans for a trip soon; we were to go to the States while friends again watched Justin, Jaden, and Daphne in Haiti. I'd tell the kids we were packing early. They could each fill suitcases with clothes and toys. If our visas were approved today, we'd be ready.

But in the flurry of the morning, I was convicted. Though I ran from one end of the hall to the other, darting in and out of the kitchen, the kids' rooms, and living room, cleaning, organizing, and packing, my mind heard the Holy Spirit's tug. This could be the biggest day of our lives. What if the sea did part? What if we got our long-awaited answer? Where would the glory go? What would the kids remember?

If my actions were in faith, I may as well go all the way. I stopped and leaned against the cement wall. *Lord, really? Should I do this?* Again, no words, no answer; but there was a peace. If God's grace was enough to sustain my own disappointed hopes at the end of the day, it would be enough for them too.

"Kids." I walked toward the girls' room, where the volume was the loudest. Sure enough, toys and clothes were flying. Everyone was there. "I have something important to tell you."

I sat on Daphne's twin bed, facing the built-in wooden wardrobe housing the girls' clothes. Brendan pulled his head out of the narrow drawer space at the bottom. The drawer had long ago broken, and now stray socks and toy trains made their home in the vacancy. "Everyone come here," I said. Brendan and Dora fought for space on my lap. Justin pelted me with questions. Daphne somersaulted on the bed and Jaden flung a jump rope back and forth across the floor.

"I told you all we need pack for our trip, right?" They nodded. "Well, I need to tell you why we're packing today." They listened in awe as I shared the possibility. This was the stuff their dreams were made of. My eight-year-old daughter, my eleven year-old sons had passed their entire lives thus far praying for this miracle. This miracle that wasn't yet realized. I needed to anchor them to reality.

"We are going to pray, kids." I looked deep into their sparkling eyes. "We're going to ask the Lord for this miracle. And if He says yes, we're going to give Him all the glory. We'll look back and remember this day and know it was all God." They nodded eagerly.

"But, I need you to listen carefully," I said. "We just don't know yet how it's going to turn out. Even if we don't get the visas to leave Haiti, we are going to know that God is good. He always knows what He's doing, okay?" I was preaching to myself.

We bowed our heads and poured out our hearts to Jesus again. My prayers had been incessant for the past two days—it wasn't like God didn't know already what I wanted, but I knew we needed to come before Him together. My kids needed this for their faith. I longed for them to seek Him, to ask, to trust, and to give Him glory in the end.

The second we uttered our amens, their chatter began. They were eager to help, finally motivated to focus—completing any chore that might speed them to an answer. All I could do was hope and pray I hadn't done the wrong thing. I couldn't imagine the sorrow of that night should our visas be denied.

A ride. How to get to Port-au-Prince was my next problem. It was unthinkable to drive myself—especially considering my recent anxiety and stress levels. Besides, I couldn't just leave our Land Cruiser in Port. A *bus*. I ran downstairs to find our tenants. They'd know about Haitian buses.

Five minutes later I was shaking my head in disbelief. What were the chances? My friends downstairs had just chartered a bus to transport supplies to Port that very night. If this was to be our exodus, I'd be traveling with friends, in a functional vehicle, with armed guards. Peace blanketed my needy soul. God saw me.

Back upstairs, I clicked my way into email. I knew I needed

to keep abreast of supply-chain progress. I scanned through the newest messages. Dixie's assistant had written. *Is this about the passport photos?* My eyes skimmed for a split second before I found myself trembling. And soon I was in that world I'd entered only a few times, that "other" world no one can enter at whim, the land of surreal, where something is so good or so bad, time is suspended. I'd been there the day I married my husband, the night thieves violated our security, the day Jarod slumped to the hospital floor as I labored to birth Dora. I blinked. I read and reread. My heart hammered.

We finally had our answer.

"Dixie just called from the Embassy. All visas have been issued. We are making arrangements for a flight that will leave tomorrow and go to Fort Lauderdale. I don't have specific details yet. But if you want the kids to be leaving Haiti, you'll need to get down here ASAP!"

I crumpled to the floor. How were there even words for this? For the answer to nine years of prayer? Where were the words of repentance for my cynicism? My doubt? My tantrums? How could I even do this moment justice? How should I share this miracle with my kids?

I knelt on the cool tile in quiet tears. *Thank you. Thank you. Thank you. I have cried out to you day after day. From this very room you have seen my heart, watched me cry, heard my prayers, known my fear. And now this.* I covered my face. *Thank you!*

I could have worshiped indefinitely. But this holy moment had to be shared. I pushed myself up and called out, hardly recognizing my own voice in my delirious fog. "Kids, come here, come here!" They came helter-skelter from their various rooms, joining me in the long narrow hall. "We're going!" They stared blankly. "We're going to the U.S.!" I cried. "We have visas for you! God has answered our prayers!"

They screamed. They jumped up and down, mouths gaping open, eyes wild. I joined them. Everyone else in the household came running. John, who'd come to visit, Leann, and finally Wilkenson. In the middle of our elation, still in the hallway, I hugged the kids close. "Let's thank God."

My heart held a thousand words of awe and praise, but all that came out were tears and an endless stream of thank yous. It was enough.

I longed to bask in the glory of answered prayer. I had a few sacred moments—the call I made to Jarod as he clung to the back of a pickup truck in the Dominican Republic, the call to my mom, the email announcement to hundreds of supporters that I could barely type for the violent shaking of my hands. But this wouldn't be a day of reflection. It was a day of action. The full load of responsibility was mine. The kids. The house. My workers. I couldn't blur out. Every detail needed my attention, and though I raced the clock, the day seemed to stretch to a millennium.

I divvied up my food, some to Leann, some to John, some to Wilkenson, some to my neighbors. I scrubbed the fridge. John too was on a quest for a visa to the United States and Canada and needed passport photos taken and printed. Jarod asked that I retrieve borrowed gas jugs from the OMS mission compound so our tenants could continue to purchase gas for our generator. I needed to return a borrowed camera. And I needed to say good-bye to many dear friends.

We piled into the Land Cruiser to run our errands, successful in some, not so successful in others. Our goodbyes were bitter-sweet. I didn't know when we'd return. I imagined we'd take a few months to complete our children's papers in the States before coming back, but there was much I didn't know. Rachelle Hubele hugged me goodbye, full of joy knowing her prayers for us had been answered. Angie Bundy, my long-time friend from OMS, wasn't even surprised when I told her we were leaving. "I saw it all last night," she said. "I saw this exact scene as I prayed for you—you coming here telling me you'd been approved. So I just thanked Him, because it was already done."

My tasks continued at a feverish pace, interjected with a few wild interruptions. On one errand, a dog bit me on my backside. All I could do was pin my torn skirt back together and pray I wouldn't get rabies! Then I received a disconcerting phone call from Dixie's daughter. She instructed me to bring my adoptive kids only, as the chartered plane would have limited space. What to do with Brendan and Dora? Despite my protest and explana-tion of Jarod's absence, she was hesitant. "You could bring them on the chance that there's room, but I can't promise anything. We have to prioritize the Haitian children. This is their only chance to get out." I was dismayed, but had to move forward.

The sun fell westward. I felt like Cinderella—my bus was to leave downtown at midnight, and I dare not miss it. My sense of safety evaporated even sooner. I called the Moores, missionary friends who lived in town near the departure spot. "Could I bring my family to your house to wait?"

"Of course."

Despite the kids' best efforts to pack their bags, I had to start over. My conversation with Dixie's daughter revealed we'd only be allowed one backpack per person. I dumped the stores of toys filling their bags to the floor and asked them to pick their two favorite items. Then we stuffed a couple outfits per child into the bags.

The shadows were falling, and I was growing frantic. *I have to leave before dark.* My panic grew exponentially at night, in the car, and when I was alone. I prayed with every breath. *Hold me together, Lord. This can't be the night I fall apart.* But the day was taking its toll on me, and I was terrified I might break down.

It was time. The kids hugged our dogs goodbye. They took their last long looks at the house and yard. Then we waved to Wilkenson, who closed the gate behind us. We would be back in a few months, we believed. But tonight we took the road forward.

# 19

## The Journey Begins

And the peace of God, which passes all understanding,
will guard your hearts and your minds in Christ Jesus.

Philippians 4:7

JANUARY 20, 2010

The Moores' house was a beacon of comfort. I parked, unloaded,
then walked into Pat's welcoming arms. She exuded the security I
needed, as did a visiting team from the States filling nearly every
corner of their home. They took my hyperactive crew into custody,
and I was able to catch a breath. My pause wasn't long though. I
had to find a way to bring my two youngest to Port.

I called all the airlines that might be able to help, hoping especially to make contact with Missionary Flights International or
Missionary Aviation Fellowship, the two missionary services airlines. But it was after business hours, and my efforts were fruitless.

My attempts to connect with the missionary flights via email were no more successful. The dial-up Internet connection was sketchy, and it seemed no one was checking email this time of day. I clung to the possibility of connecting in the morning, maybe even at the airport. Surely someone would have enough heart and space on a flight to help my kids get out of Haiti with me. For tonight though, I'd have to let it go.

While I'd passed a couple hours on the phone, Daphne had contracted fever and the stomach flu. *Really, Lord? Vomiting and diarrhea on a bus ride?* I soothed her the best I could, and begged God for relief before midnight.

Then came an email from Dixie's assistant: "Be sure to bring all your adoption paperwork."

My heart sank. While I'd thought to bring birth certificates for the kids, I'd believed the visas Dixie had secured were all we'd need. With such limited luggage space, I hadn't thought to bring the mountain of documents that to me seemed so worthless. And now I'd have to drive back home.

I decided to take Brendan. His exhaustion was manifesting itself in uncontrollable craziness. The others seemed sleepy, content to remain with Pat and the team. Thankfully, a close friend of ours, Enoch, was willing to drive me back out. I almost cried in relief.

Brendan was asleep after only a few minutes on the rough road. Fifteen minutes later, we pulled into our yard. Enoch volunteered to stay with Brendan in the car while I retrieved my paperwork. I pushed my jitters aside, unlocking the front door and flooding the house with light. I restarted the desktop computer to send a hurried note to Jarod, hoping, praying he'd check email at his Dominican hotel, even though it was late. "Should I risk taking Dora and Brendan?" I rose to gather all the documents I'd need.

I'd never been great at organizing paperwork, and tonight I regretted my lack of discipline. I knew we had the papers, I just had to unearth them from various drawers, shelves, and folders. A lot of things were written in French; some were outdated and some had been renewed. It was hard, especially in my frenzied state, to know which things were pertinent and which were unnecessary. I'd have to take them all. I filled a computer satchel with them, dismayed I'd have another heavy bag to shoulder, but unwilling to risk leaving anything I might need.

I checked my email again, thankful to find a response from Jarod. I scanned as fast as I could:

"I'm willing to leave my work and pick Brendan and Dora up in Cap tomorrow if you want to leave them behind."

I heaved a sigh. We both realized that this would jeopardize several supply runs. Who knew how long it would take him to get back to the relief work if we went through with this plan? I rubbed my temples. My head ached from the strain of the day and now the burden of this decision.

Enoch sprinted up the stairs, startling me out of my thoughts. "We really need to go. It's not safe to be out so late." I'd wanted to await Jarod's final decision, but if this six-foot-four Haitian man was concerned for our security, I knew I should listen. I shut down the computer, grabbed my bag, and followed Enoch. Pausing at the stairway for just a moment though, I looked down the hall, absorbing all the memories, good and bad. We'd fought thieves and birthed a baby here. Killed rats, planned a wedding, nearly lost our minds. God had been here with us. But now it seemed His pillar of fire was guiding us elsewhere. *Goodbye sweet home.*

Safely back in town, I received another email from Jarod. He decided he'd do it: Leave the Dominican Republic the next day. I was to leave Dora and Brendan with Pat, to be picked up by other missionary friends in the morning. He'd claim them the following afternoon, then fly them to the States as soon as he could book a flight.

I knew it could work, and it wasn't the end of the world for us, though the kids would feel it was. But Jarod was the only one in the Dominican Republic authorized to handle donated funds. The supply train would be placed on hold until he returned. And that could actually mean the end of the world for the clinics and individuals counting on food, water, and electricity.

But this was his decision, and I determined to honor it. *Give me strength to do this, God. Or if you still want to change things, help us both understand.*

It was time to wake the kids. They'd need to use the restroom one final time and gather their bags. The bus would pick us up in fifteen minutes.

Brendan was too far gone to wake, but Dora opened her bleary eyes. "Honey, I need you to listen carefully." I braced myself. She was going to hate me. "There's not room on the airplane for you and Brendan to go with us, but Daddy is going to come get you tomorrow and bring you on another plane in a few days."

Her eyes filled with horror, then tears. She clung to me for dear life. This was totally not working. The middle of the night was hardly the time for reasonable conversations with six-year-old girls. Who was I kidding? I was in an even more fragile emotional state than she was. I honestly didn't think I could make myself leave my two babies.

In one last-ditch effort, I reopened my laptop. My fingers flew. "Jarod, Dora is sobbing, I'm a wreck, and I can't even get Brendan to wake up for me to explain. I think I should take everyone, since they said they'll do all they can to fit us on the plane. And I know you shouldn't leave your work—there's too much at stake. Our bus comes in a few minutes. Write back quick!"

Daphne was a limp rag. She clutched plastic bags in case she'd vomit on the bus ride. Jaden and Justin were awake and alert for the moment. Brendan was still in his sleep coma, and Dora was a tear-stained disaster. We sat near the door, waiting for our ride, praying Jarod's email response would arrive before the bus. *Come on, come on . . . write back!* I clicked "check mail" again and again, praying the connection wouldn't fail.

Finally it came: "Okay, go, and I'll pray like crazy!"

I hugged Dora close. "It's okay, honey. Daddy says we should all go. You're coming with us."

She buried her wet face in my shoulder, and I breathed a prayer of gratitude.

The bus came at midnight. There were a few unknown faces as well as Joann, our downstairs tenant, and Emmanuel, our deportee friend. I hugged Pat goodbye, then surveyed the bus interior. It was beautiful compared to the traditional Haitian buses. I was told a few of these had been a gift from the United

States to the mayor of Cap. We'd be traveling in a caravan, each of these sleek white buses rented out by individuals or organizations bringing supplies to Port and rescuing loved ones. Bags of rice and beans and jugs of diesel lined the aisle. The seats were hard, but comfortably shaped and clean. There was air-conditioning and panoramic windows. Best of all, these buses didn't look like they were at death's door. And even if they did break down, the presence of a mechanic on each bus ensured we wouldn't be stuck for long.

I arranged my kids as best I could. I laid Jaden over the double seat across the aisle, Justin sat with Emmanuel, and Daphne lay down in the seat diagonal from me. I kept hold of Brendan and Dora. Thankfully we'd brought pillows. I knew we wouldn't be able to bring them on the plane—if space was limited, I didn't want to push our luck. But we could use them tonight, then donate them to the orphanage to which our bus's supplies were going.

The bus pulled away from the Moores' house, then joined its companions in the city square, where each was outfitted with an armed guard. Already there were too many stories of robberies along this route. No one wanted to take chances.

I had hoped I might get a few hours' sleep en route, but those hopes were quickly dashed. The speed we traveled at combined with the condition of the road meant I'd spend the night as a human cushion. I braced myself to remain upright, balancing so as not to drop Brendan or push Dora off her seat. Justin and Daphne managed to right themselves after potholes knocked them off their seats, but Jaden was the worst off. Each violent lurch sent him to the floor. And each time his head, knee, or elbow cracked against the seat or floor, he'd cry out, then struggle to get back up. I was helpless to support him, with two other bodies to protect, so I finally summoned the nerve to rouse a stranger in a seat nearby. "Sir, could I trouble you to help my son? He keeps falling." To my relief, he obliged.

My stomach churned as we made our way up the mountains. This was the most treacherous part of the trip. The ravines only inches from my window were enough to chill my blood in broad daylight with my trusted husband at the wheel.

The views were breathtakingly beautiful though too. The moon shone over the curves, the peaks, and the jagged drops. It was dazzling. *Look up, Jen, not down. The Maker of all this is with you.* I tried to relax. He'd answered our prayers and led us this far. Though my nerves were primed to panic, I determined to trust. It wasn't easy—there was a new fear every few moments of this journey that stretched on and on and on. But never before had I felt what I began to feel now: *peace that passed understanding.* The very moment a fresh anxiety arose, a Scripture rose to defeat it. The instant my heart started to pound, a song of praise rose to my lips. *People are praying.* I knew it, and for once it was almost palpable. Though I wouldn't get more than a few blinks of sleep, I was reminded that God would hold me together.

My phone buzzed. Jarod had added minutes to my cell phone from the Dominican Republic. A few minutes later, my phone rang. Nick Hobgood, our scuba diving friend, offered to put me in touch with coworkers in Port if I needed help getting to the airport. I was encouraged. This all just might work out.

*Now, if only I could figure out a way to help Jaden go to the bathroom!*

The bus had already made a roadside stop, but I hadn't been able to wake him. Now he was desperate. It was still dark; everyone was asleep. I just couldn't ask the driver to pull over again so soon. I racked my brain and finally came up with a plan. *Desperate times call for desperate measures.* Jaden and I slid our way down the bus aisle, now slick with diesel spills. Making our way to the back of the bus, we turned a back corner and a ziplock bag into a restroom. We threw it out the window, stumbled back to our seats, and journeyed on.

Daylight broke as we made our way down to the plains. The light of sunrise revealed a depressing sight—a wrecked bus. Travelers coming out of Port had collided with an SUV. We slowed, able to take in the scene without stopping. It seemed the injured were receiving help, and perhaps no one had been killed. Yet still, I knew the bus had been loaded with earthquake survivors, headed out of Port to rejoin family and friends up north. I felt their trauma upon trauma even as they faded from our view. *That's how it is here.* I squeezed my eyes shut. *Mountain after mountain.* The Creole proverb was all too true.

The kids stirred from their sleep, instantly hungry. I doled out the granola bars and peanut butter sandwiches Pat sent along. Jaden wanted nothing to do with them. His idea of a meal was nothing short of three cups of steaming rice and beans. *It's going to be a long day for you, buddy.* I dreaded how frustrated he was bound to become.

I looked back at Daphne. Her eyes were open, and she didn't

look great, but she was ready to drink. "Here you go, sweetie." I handed her some water. "I'm so glad you didn't throw up during the night!"

"I did." Her words were still weak.

"Oh! I'm so sorry! Where's the bag?"

She stared blankly. Then said, "I forgot about the bags."

We both looked down at the floor in horror. But somehow the diesel and the constant swaying of the bus had wiped out any trace of incriminating mess.

The other three, still sleepy and fairly quiet, munched their breakfast as stunning beaches began to line the coast on the east. We weren't far from Port now. Back in our first year here, we'd come to this very beach resort, where Jaden had taken a bite out of his glass. The waters were every shade of crystal blue and turquoise, the very picture of refreshment. I drank the beauty in, wanting to store it away against the devastation that was sure to meet my eyes in only a few miles.

The outskirts of Port looked normal—the kind of normal that had always looked like earthquake rubble. Unfinished cement block structures, piles of trash, mounds of rocks. This wasn't out of the ordinary yet. But several miles further led us to fields lined with tents. Fear of crumbling houses kept many in these new tent cities. And naturally, those whose regular shelter had never been as nice as these tents got in on the donations from relief workers as well. I imagined it was hard for charities to know where to start and where to stop. It had to be nearly impossible for them to tell who was an actual earthquake victim and who suffered from chronic poverty.

It was eight in the morning now. I decided I'd better call Dixie and let her know we were in town. After several unsuccessful tries, we established a staticky connection. I told her I'd take our bus to the U.S. Consulate, where Nick had arranged a connection for me. I'd catch a ride from there to the airport. She said her caravan of eighty would be heading down the mountains of Petionville soon and would meet us there.

"And Jennifer," she said, "here's the tail number of our plane."

I jotted it down. *So far so good.*

Another hour ticked by. Once we hit downtown, the traffic slowed to a crawl. There were few roads available to motorists, and everyone with a car had important errands. Besides the cars, the roadside was a flurry of pedestrians. I wondered what each person's story was, how many miracles and tragedies passed by my window.

I began to see the damage, though we only skirted the edges of the worst areas. How many had perished in these fallen homes and businesses? Even yesterday's aftershock may have played a part in what I was seeing.

The reminder of aftershocks sent a shudder through my body. There was simply no telling when more might hit, no guarantee of safety. I didn't realize it yet, but the entire country would be fighting varying degrees of post-traumatic stress, one element of which was the certainty that some other disaster lurked just around the corner. I, along with everyone else, was waiting for the other shoe to drop. The worst part of it was, this was the land where it almost always did.

We inched our way toward the Consulate, stopping once to

get gas and take a much-needed bathroom break. Back in the bus, I called Nick's friend at USAID to ask her to meet us in a half hour. But despite my repeated attempts to communicate, she couldn't hear me.

"We'll look for you in a few minutes," I heard her say. As traffic slowed to a complete stop, I feared we'd miss her completely.

"How far do you think we are?" I asked the driver.

"Less than a mile."

I looked at my kids and our luggage, weighing the options. The pedestrians out our windows were passing all the vehicles. *We could walk that far, right? Especially if it means making our connection.*

I hated making decisions. I'd have given anything to have Jarod beside me, calling the shots and shouldering the responsibility, but today it was all on me.

"Okay." I took a deep breath. "Kids, we're going have to get out and walk."

We gathered some food and water, slung our backpacks on, and stepped out onto the street. The heat threatened to sap what energy I had, but if we were going to make it through this chaos, I'd have to be strong. Cars and taptaps honked as pedestrians shouldered through the traffic jam.

I had to yell to the kids to make myself heard. "Justin, hold hands with Dora and Jaden. I'll carry Brendan, and hang on to Daphne." I looked at my wilting daughter. She was still feverish and could barely hold herself up. My shoulders sagged when I realized I was asking far too much of her.

Just then, Emmanuel bounded out of the bus. "I'll carry Daphne for you. I can run back to the bus after I help you get to the Consulate."

He led the way, speeding along. We lagged behind, weighed down by my luggage and slower kids. A man walking beside us noticed our difficulties. "Let me carry that for you." He gestured to my bags. Any other day, I'd have refused, cynically or maybe realistically believing an offer to help was a chance to be robbed. But today was different.

"Thank you." I shifted my load onto his shoulder and repositioned Brendan on my hip.

"How are things going for you and your family?" I asked him as we wove our way down the street. His story was one of loss, of course. I listened to his sorrow as we closed the gap between the bus and the Consulate. Upon reaching my destination, he handed me my bag.

"Mèsi." I was so grateful for his kindness. Contrary to the norm, he hadn't asked this "blan" for any payment. "God bless you."

He left, and I looked up at the entrance. Emmanuel stood a few feet away, also taking in the scene. Something wasn't right. A hundred people were lined up, and American soldiers guarded a perimeter around the building.

"Excuse me, sir!" I approached one of the soldiers. "We're here to meet someone at the Consulate."

"It's closed, Ma'am," he said, then spun around to attend to the crowd.

*No, this can't be!* Panic welled in an instant. *I was just talking with Nick's friend. She would've told me if they were closing!*

I took a few steps down to the next solder. "Sir! My children and I are supposed meet someone inside. Can you let us in?"

"I'm so sorry, Ma'am," he said. "No one's allowed in. The Consulate has just closed."

I stared, unbelieving. This couldn't be happening. I couldn't be stranded with all my kids now! I had to get in there. I opened my mouth for one last plea, but he spoke again, dashing any remaining hope.

"We're about to turn all these people away, Ma'am, and it's not going to be pretty. If I was you, I'd get out of here as quickly as possible."

# 20

## On Dry Land

He turned the sea into dry land

Psalm 66:6

JANUARY 21, 2010

I stepped back in defeat. Justin, understanding the situation's gravity, looked at me in dismay. I met his gaze. "Okay, we need to pray." With eyes open, I shot up yet another plea for divine intervention.

*USAID. Ask the soldier about that.*

There was only one entrance as far as I could see, and if the soldier said the building was closed, I didn't know what difference it would make, but I decided to give it a try. I stepped forward once more.

"Excuse me, sir. I actually need to see someone in the USAID department. Do you think I could find someone from their office to speak with?"

"Oh." His countenance changed. "Yes, Ma'am. That's not a problem. Come this way." I was taken aback. *Was it really that simple?* Thank God I hadn't just walked away!

The soldier waited a moment for me to get Daphne out of Emmanuel's arms and corral my kids toward the entrance gate. I threw a last glance over my shoulder. "Thank you, Emmanuel!" And we were ushered inside.

We placed our bags on a conveyor belt to be scanned. How strange to step instantly into an American environment, complete with security protocols. Justin and Daphne were intrigued by the process—they'd never experienced this before. Once we'd passed under the scanner, a receptionist attempted to reach Nick's friend. We took turns on the only two seats in the lobby and waited. Forty-five minutes slid by, and still we couldn't make contact. As a couple employees came into view from an adjoining hallway, I recognized a woman Nick and Dina had introduced us to a few weeks back.

"Do I know you?" I asked as she neared us. "I think we met at the Hobgood's house."

She grinned. "Yes! I remember you. Are you the one I'm supposed to help?"

I sighed in relief. "Yes! I've been trying and trying to reach you!"

She hugged me, apologizing for the poor phone connection. "I was just heading home. Come with us, and my friend David here will drive you to the airport." They escorted us outside to the parking lot.

We threw our bags into the back of his pickup, then squeezed into the cab. Everyone was too tightly packed to lie down, but within a mile, every single kid had nodded off. I was jealous. My eyes stung from lack of sleep, but I was determined to stay alert. Again, traffic kept us from making much progress. We'd been driving for over an hour when I spotted the airport entrance Dixie had instructed me to use.

"Here's our stop," I said to David.

"No, we can't go in there," he said. "You have to use the main entrance."

I was skeptical, but we'd already missed the turn. *I guess we'll find out.*

Fifteen minutes later, I was proved right. And thirty minutes later found us back at the correct exit. *This is just how things are going to go today,* I sighed inwardly. Then I corrected myself. *What am I thinking? It's how things go in Haiti all the time!* Regardless, we'd arrived. And this was where our exodus was to take place. Being here was a miracle, no matter how complicated.

I roused the kids. "We're at the airport! Let's go."

We gathered our luggage, our driver took off, and we were left surveying the sights and sounds before us. I could hardly hear myself think, the drone of the planes, mostly military, were so deafening. There was a small airport about a mile off to our right. It shared a runway with the international airport, which was only a quarter mile to our left. I'd never entered here before; it was a side entrance to the runway and tarmac. Dixie had warned me about the airport that morning—the building had structural damage and had been deemed unsafe. We'd have to wait outside. Judging by the flurry of activity, and passengers preparing for outbound flights toward our left, that's where we belonged.

Ours was a slow caravan. I didn't have any extra help for Daphne this time, so we paused frequently to rest. When we finally reached the back side of the airport, we were ready to sit. I looked around. There were a few areas with folding chairs, roped off for traveling military personnel, but other than that, no seating whatsoever. There was no sign of Dixie and her eighty children yet. All we could do was sit on the cement and wait.

We plopped down among a smattering of individuals, mostly news teams and relief workers, on the tarmac. Daphne collapsed on the one pillow I'd allowed her to smuggle along. I stroked her cheek and offered her more water.

The rest of the kids were hungry, even though it wasn't quite eleven in the morning. I dug through my bag. "Hot dogs, anyone?" They were straight from the package, with no accompanying condiments, but the kids didn't even fuss. They washed them down with our last bit of water, leading me to wonder how we'd remain hydrated for the rest of the day. Though a trip through the international airport was normally filled with tasty temptations from the restaurant inside, today there weren't even vendors or snack stands. I'd been warned it would be like this. Port-au-Prince residents were struggling to find enough drinking water for themselves, let alone enough to sell along the street or in stores. I prayed that water would somehow turn up.

There was absolutely nothing for the kids to do. I'd been so strict with their luggage that they had no books, electronics, or even drawing supplies. After the novelty of watching planes wore off, they entertained themselves with random bits of trash from the ground. I knew the bottle caps and scraps of metal were completely unsanitary, but it was worth my sanity to let them play.

Then came the moment I'd been dreading. "Mom, I have to go to the bathroom."

As dehydrated as everyone was, we were still going to have to find a restroom. I hadn't seen any. I didn't feel good about leaving anyone unattended while I searched one out, so the lot of us traipsed around until we found porta-potties up near the entrance.

The hours passed slowly. We received a bit of a reprieve when a neighborly Frenchman provided us with the prayed-for bottled water. We continued our walks between our luggage and the bathrooms, my eyes constantly peeled for Dixie. I was sure she should have been there by now. I'd called her husband, who was back at their orphanage, and he's assured me she'd left long ago. The shadows were lengthening, and I couldn't imagine that she'd want to cut things so close when she had eighty-three children to process before our departure. Something didn't feel right. *Maybe she'd had car trouble?* But aside from calling her cell—which I'd attempted repeatedly, to no avail—I had no choice other than to wait.

Six o'clock came, the time Dixie had told me they'd hoped to leave. The sky was darkening. I'd read tail numbers for hours, relieved that our plane seemingly hadn't left without us, but uneasy that, from what I could tell, it hadn't arrived either. By this time most of the other travelers were gone. My heart rate increased with each passing minute, then doubling when shouts erupted around us. A thief, followed by a cop, sprinted through our dwindling camp.

"We're getting out of here, kids." I jumped to my feet, fighting an anxiety attack. "Quick! Everyone, follow me."

We shuffled along as fast as we could, me on my phone, trying, trying, trying to reach Dixie. I approached a small group of marines. "Excuse me, would you be able to help me figure out if I've missed my plane?" I gave one of the men the tail number, bracing myself to hear the worst.

"It doesn't look like this plane has arrived yet, Ma'am," he said after checking some records. "Do you need some help?"

I explained my dilemma, and he offered to drive his jeep around to search for Dixie's group. The kids and I waited, weary and limp as the sun disappeared completely. After more futile attempts to reach Dixie's cell, I tried her husband's number again.

"I don't know where they are. They should be right there," he said. "But here's another number you can try. It's her assistant's cell."

I hung up, and my phone beeped. *No!* My battery would soon be dead.

I dialed her assistant a few times. *Please, God.* Finally, there was a voice on the other end. "Hello. This is Brad."

"Brad! Are you with Dixie?"

"Yes."

"This is Jennifer Ebenhack. Where are you?"

"At the airport—the small one."

I wanted to scream, my relief quickly switching to anger. But all I could do was ask in a shaky voice if he could please come pick us up.

Another twenty minutes passed before he found us. Ironically, when we saw each other, we realized we were well acquainted from his previous work in Cap Haitian. And Justin blurted, "Mom! I told you I saw Brad Reimer a few hours ago!" We'd seen him and had waved, but hadn't caught his attention, and he'd passed on by. I sighed. It was over. I couldn't change anything now.

We drove to the small airport, where Dixie's crew was sprawled on blankets on a grassy hill. It was all festivity over here. Toddlers, babies, and a few older kids danced and babbled and sang. A few adoptive parents had come to Haiti to help escort them to the United States. Dixie's staff darted in and out of the chaos, feeding kids, holding babies, and changing diapers. The stars twinkled overhead, and my fears were finally allowed to evaporate. We'd made it. I could have punched someone—*anyone*—to rid myself of the frustration that had built up all day, but Dixie's welcoming hug took the edge off my aggravation. "We looked for you at the Consulate, and tried to reach you by phone," she said, "but I had eighty kids to care for, so all I could do was pray for God to bring you here in time!"

"Well, thank goodness He did," I said, smiling. *None too soon, either!*

After another thirty minutes of mingling with the crowd, we were informed the plane had arrived. Everyone was bused to the runway to meet the chartered 737. I looked for its tail number through the bus window. *It's not even on there!* My heart skipped a beat, realizing I would have never recognized it had we even seen it from our previous spot. Additionally, the location where we boarded would have been hidden from view. We'd made contact with Brad just in time.

The bus parked, and we walked through the damp night air to the plane. With each ascending stair to the plane, my kids stepped further away from the Haitian land that had birthed them. We were sure we'd be back, but I was ready for a break.

A few days ago, Dixie had mentioned the possibility of flying in the belly of a military cargo plane. I looked around at the plush seats and air vents on this Vision Airline plane. What a relief to be here instead. The kids and I took seats and belted up. Justin was thrilled with the anticipation of his first jet ride. Daphne, always fearful of heights, wasn't too sure. Jaden, well, he just lived in the moment.

My panic was gone, but as the other children and caregivers filed onto the plane, I began to wonder if there would truly be enough room for everyone. *Surely Dora and Brendan are safe at this point. . . .* When Dixie herself came aboard, I called her over to double check.

She leaned over the seat. "You know what? There was supposed to be a medical team of thirty people joining us in chartering this plane. It should have been full. But we just received word that they aren't going to leave tonight. There is plenty of room for your kids."

My sleepy eyes were instantly moist. *Thank you, Jesus.*

I tried to call Jarod with my last minute of battery, but he didn't answer. I got through to Nick though, and asked him to email Jarod that all was well. With that, my phone shut itself off.

Babies and toddlers fussed as the airline crew prepared for takeoff. A voice came over the loudspeaker: "We'd ask that you make sure there is at least one adult in each row." *Not your typical announcement*, I thought, smiling to myself. I looked behind me. The plane looked empty, since most of the passengers weren't tall enough to see over the seat backs.

That realization opened a floodgate of emotion. Our three kids represented years of effort, prayers, and emotional investment, not to mention thousands of dollars. But there were *eighty more kids* on this plane. That meant dozens of families were receiving the answers to their prayers tonight. This *was* the opening of another Red Sea. Corruption hadn't won this battle. In the aftermath of a tragedy, little girls and boys were going home to moms and dads whose hearts were breaking for them. This was a miracle.

I looked at my own kids. I would have given anything for the camera Jarod had taken to the Dominican Republic—for a way to memorialize this sacred moment. *Our kids, leaving Haiti at last.* It was so different than I'd ever imagined, but so incredible. *His ways are higher than our ways.*

We lifted into the sky at eleven at night. Our planeload, a nursery in the air, quickly quieted. Only a few whimpers were heard in the next hour and a half. At twelve thirty, darkness gave way to the sparkling lights of Miami International Airport. Never had I been so elated to reach American soil. I had dreamt of this moment for nine whole years. I'd imagined it on our first visit to Haiti, so sure we'd eventually escort two toddlers back to our Moody apartment, downtown Chicago. I'd hoped and prayed for it on our way to the States, when proof of infertility seemed within arms' reach. And how many other times had I begged, pleaded, fasted . . . clinging to the vision of three brown faces lighting with the joy of a family Christmas, dancing at the first touch of snow on their warm cheeks, running through a wheat field, an Arizona desert, a park, a playground. And now those things were coming! A whole new world of delight was soon to unfold.

But it wasn't really the material stuff. It wasn't about location. It wasn't the American Dream.

It was about staying together. This land would make our family official, as we'd prayed for so long. We'd be united by law, not just by heart.

It was the fulfilling of a promise. The promise that was a shadow of our eternal adoptions to come. A promise that the orphaned and abandoned will always belong. That they are treasured and can never be ripped out of our lives. We are bound together.

Tears blurred my view of the airport as we skidded to a stop and taxied to the jet bridge.

"We're here kids," I murmured, voice trembling. "We've crossed over on dry ground. We made it to the U.S.!"

# 21

## Strengthened

The LORD will guide you always;
he will satisfy your needs in a sun-scorched land
and will strengthen your frame.

Isaiah 58:11 NIV


JANUARY 22, 2010

It was surreal—watching my children take their first steps into the United States. Grateful tears threatened to pour from my eyes, as airport employees, lining the jet-bridge, applauded our arrival. Jaden managed to trip his way into his new country, but in an instant was scooped up by a helpful employee into a wheelchair. My kids grinned as they watched, delighted with the solution this place was able to provide so quickly.

We spent that night, my second without real sleep, in the airport. All eighty-three children had to be documented in Immigration—no small ordeal for Dixie. As our caravan of kids passed eight hours in one glassed-in room, airport personnel continued to ease our discomfort, distributing diapers, formula, snacks, coffee, coloring books, and stuffed animals. America made an endearing first impression on all.

By eight in the morning, each child had been granted humanitarian parole, allowing families two years to complete their children's U.S. adoptions. The I-95 forms in my hand were pure gold—a treasure sought through blood, sweat, and tears, yet won purely by grace. Each event following—a television interview, a reunion with dear friends, and especially the welcome-home party in Wichita's airport the next day—was an overflow of this blessing. Every moment was unforgettable, to be cherished for a lifetime. We'd made it to the other side of our dreams. We'd been given our hearts' desires.

Everything swirled into place. Jarod arrived in Kansas a few weeks later, when Samaritan's Purse took the reins of the relief work he and Matt McCormick had begun. And the day of complete official victory was the twentieth of September, 2010, when the court of Newton, Kansas at last pronounced the adoptions of Justin, Jaden, and Daphne Ebenhack.

We mailed adoption announcements to friends and family, bearing testimony to the miracle we never could have foreseen at the start of the process, nine years earlier. Beneath the pictures of our three adopted children, I included the words of Psalm 66:5-6, which I'd read on the final flight with the kids from Florida to Kansas:

> Come and see what God has done:
>> he is awesome in his deeds toward the children of man.

> He turned the sea into dry land;
>> they passed through the river on foot.
> There did we rejoice in him.

Shortly following our children's adoptions, we learned that a return to Haiti's corruption could jeopardize the adoptions—something we simply could not risk. As we realized our life and ministry would now be in the United States, I felt I'd been granted a new freedom—permission for a safe existence after this parting of the waters.

"Happily ever after" seemed within reach.

But the panic I'd experienced in Haiti didn't disappear. Weeks passed, then months, and still I struggled. As anxiety attacks struck in new settings, I developed more phobias. I longed to avoid the places and situations that increased my discomfort, but was always careful to project a healthy, normal image to others. I began to feel dissociated from my own body, as if the voice, thoughts, and actions I performed weren't even connected to the real me. My symptoms fit the description of depersonalization, a disorder frequently brought on by trauma.

I was in less danger than ever before, yet tormented in a way I'd not yet experienced. I was afraid I was going crazy, yet equally afraid any kind of treatment would be worse than my problems.

It was a new desert. I'd crossed the sea, and while still singing my song of victory, I found myself in another kind of wilderness. I was weary. I begged God—who had just yesterday done these great things—for healing in this new scorched place.

Not knowing what else to do, I clung, needier than ever, to Jesus. I didn't have the ability to fully articulate these strange feelings to those around me; after all, I didn't even understand them myself. So again, I made God my refuge. In the darkness, He was my pillar of fire, and through each day, the cloud that led my way. Out on errands, I would find myself gripping the handle of a shopping cart, focusing on the reality of Jesus even while everything else turned fuzzy. Then, as I panicked in the darkness of my bedroom each night, I would beg Him for help, claiming the peace that passes understanding. Once more, I was walking in the mysterious tension between misery and intimacy. I would have given anything to return to a normal state of mind and health, yet I felt myself pushing roots deep into God's nourishing soil, knowing good could come of this. *If I survived.* I wasn't completely sure that I would.

But the Lord drew my gaze to the plaque, right there in our borrowed home in Newton, Kansas, bearing words from Isaiah 58:11. I read and reread the surrounding verses, my soul crying out again for grace. My frame needed strength. I longed for the Lord's guidance.

My healing wasn't miraculous or ethereal. It didn't come that instant as hope was revived. But the Holy Spirit urged me to seek wisdom, find answers, to be humble enough to ask for help.

And He provided that help. Through a holistic physician, I found I was suffering from adrenal fatigue, a disorder of a depleted adrenal system, manifested in my life through extreme fatigue, panic, and anxiety. It was the natural physical reaction to all I'd experienced as everyday life. Through Christian counseling services, I was able to work through posttraumatic stress and process the everyday stresses of the past eight years. Thanks to my patient, loving husband and extended family, I found understanding, encouragement, and motivation to press on. By God's grace, healing slowly worked its way through my mind, body, and soul. Again, my God saw me, strengthened me, and guided me.

After eighteen months of struggle and recovery in Kansas, Jarod and I knew it was time to move on to new areas of ministry. While the door to Haiti was closed for our family, there were other ways to impact Haiti's people. In the summer of 2012, we moved to South Florida—the closest thing to Haiti we could find without leaving the country—where we now teach, coach, write, homeschool, and go through life side-by-side with many Haitian friends.

We are blessed. We're on the other side of our Red Sea. But though the United States provides more comfort, it's still a desert, not the ultimate promised land. Each member of our family is a broken person in a fallen world, and our journey continues. *Dèyè monn gen monn*—Beyond the mountains, more mountains.

We each have our own issues, fresh challenges, and new mountains to face. Some days we shudder, some days we ask the burning "why?" that every human heart cries.

But we are never forsaken.

None of us are.

Our God is no taptap driver, mindless of our pain or heavy load. No, He offers to carry our burdens, to give rest to our weary souls. For the weight of our sin, He offers eternal forgiveness through faith in Jesus. For the brokenness sin brings to this world and to our lives, He provides sufficient grace. And for all those living parched lives, He offers hope. The refreshment He extends is available to any who accept it. As Jeremiah 17:5b-8 states:

Cursed is the man who trusts in man
   and makes flesh his strength,
   whose heart turns away from the Lord.
He is like a shrub in the desert,
   and shall not see any good come.
He shall dwell in the parched places of the wilderness,
   in an uninhabited salt land.

Blessed is the man who trusts in the Lord,
   whose trust is the Lord.
He is like a tree planted by water,
   that sends out its roots by the stream,
and does not fear when heat comes,
   for its leaves remain green,
and is not anxious in the year of drought,
   for it does not cease to bear fruit.

We are seen and loved by Jesus. We're invited to trust Him; to trust the One who provides nourishment even in the driest of seasons, to trust the only One who can produce fruit even during the drought.

This God who sustains life and renews strength is the Author of all our stories. Though the characters, plots, and details differ, He will never stop writing stories of grace through our lives: stories of springs in the desert, of the abandoned set in families, of the broken made whole. Stories of hope in sun-scorched lands.

# Afterword

For more of Jennifer's story about anxiety, post traumatic stress, and adrenal fatigue, look for *Take Courage: Choosing faith on my journey of fear* on amazon.com and barnesandnoble.com.

To read more from Jennifer, contact her, or set up speaking engagements, visit jenniferebenhack.com.

# Acknowledgments

After one of the many letdowns in the adoption process, I stood, sweltering, hanging laundry in our backyard. *Lord*, I prayed silently, *this saga is just unbelievable. It's almost as if you're orchestrating it, like your setting us up for something really big.* For a second there, I was sure of it: *He's going to do something miraculous.* My next thought was: *When He does, I'll write a book about it!*

That moment and my calm belief got swallowed up in the roller coaster ride of the days, months, and years to follow. But now, on the other side of that miracle, I want to thank God for His good and perfect plan for my family and for this book. *Lord Jesus, this was all about you, and I want to give you the glory for every part. Apart from you I can do nothing.*

Jarod, my gracious husband, and Justin, Jaden, Daphne, Dora, and Brendan, thank you for praying for me as I wrote over the past five years. And thank you for rejoicing with me as I completed this book. Thank you too for the hours you let me get away to write in peace and quiet! I know it meant some extra craziness for you at home, but you were truly wonderful and didn't complain. I love you all!

And to the many others who have walked this journey with my family and me, I thank you dearly:

Mom, you nurtured me, trained me in God's ways, then let me go. Since then, you've listened, supported, encouraged and prayed. Thank you for always pointing me back to God—through every event of this book and through the writing of it as well.

Grandma and Papa, you've invested in my life in every way. Thank you for your generosity to my family and me, for loving us, and for showing me that writing a book is entirely possible!

Jonathan and Jeremy Jordan, you are the best brothers ever. Thank you for your support through our years in Haiti, for always offering a listening ear, and for investing in my family and this book in so many ways.

Uncle Glenn and Uncle Sid Litke, each of you poured into my life in special and unique ways, but both of you encouraged me to dream God's dreams, whether that be studying at Moody, going to the mission field, or writing. Thank you for loving and supporting me so fully.

Tom and Janie Ebenhack, thank you for parenting my wonderful husband. He has followed God's leading into some wild situations, and loved me and our kids in amazing ways. Your influence is a huge part of that. Thank you too for being so incredibly supportive of our family through every crazy turn of this adventure we're living.

Jamie Marner, you have been a blessing and encouragement from Chicago times till the present. Thank you for praying me through every kind of day as I wrote this book. You have never stopped believing God wanted me to write this story. I'm deeply grateful for the friendship God's given us.

Ruth Pirrie, you were the first writer friend to give me hope that this book could really happen. Thank you for the gift of your encouraging words. God used you to impact me and the entire direction of my life in a huge way.

Sarah Saville, my first Florida friend, you were enthusiastic about my book from the first moment you heard me dream aloud. Thank you for caring, listening, and even making some of these chapters happen through babysitting, coffees, meals, and prayers!

Amy Allen—and yes, Steve too—you've heard more of my triumphs and tragedies than any friend or neighbor should have to endure! But you have listened, loved, and prayed through it all over the past few years, blessing me more than you'll ever know.

Becky Finch, your gorgeous design work is just a tiny reflection of your beautiful heart. Thank you for sharing your talent and time with me. Your friendship and your belief in this project have refreshed my heart again and again.

Lisa Jacobson, I marvel at the role you played in bringing this book about. Thank you for reading my ebook and then speaking with that literary agent husband of yours about my memoir! I'm so grateful for the many ways you've encouraged me—honoring me with your foreword, welcoming me into the Club31Women family, not to mention blessing my heart with a joy and warmth that stretches all the way from Oregon to Florida.

Matt Jacobson, I so appreciate your support, patience, and wisdom through every stage of this book's development. Thank you for transitioning from my agent to my publisher, and for believing God would use this for His glory.

Jeff Reimer, your edits were a great help and blessing. Thank you for jumping into this project, making it better, and encouraging me along the way.

Gretchen Louise, thank you for working out the details of publishing. What a blessing to hand this over to an enthusiastic expert!

Michelle Shingleton, you made photo shoots fun. Thank you for your patience with me, my family, and my ideas. It all turned out beautifully.

Gillian Marchenko, Julie Brasington, and Trina Holden, thank you for your gracious endorsements and life-giving words.

To the dear missionaries whose lives intertwined with ours during our years in Haiti: Thank you for blessing us, for truly being our family in a difficult place. For those of you who continue to make Haiti your home, we pray for God's strength and grace to sustain and empower you. Thank you for your faithful service to Him!

I also want to thank the many supporters who made our ministry in Haiti possible. You were so generous, constantly giving, so we could follow God's call. May the Lord meet your needs and bless you beyond what you can ask or imagine.

And to our professors of Moody Bible Institute, those who prepared us for the challenges of cross-cultural ministry, *thank you!* Your lives, your stories, your teaching, and your hearts for God made a deep impact on Jarod and me and countless others.

Siliana and Veneste, we love you and the sweet children you birthed. Thank you for entrusting them to us. Our prayer for you:

> The Lord bless you and keep you;
> the Lord make his face to shine upon you
> and be gracious to you;
> the Lord lift up his countenance upon you
> and give you peace.
> Numbers 6:24-26

# About the Author

Jennifer's first eighteen years were
filled with family, farm life, music,
and godly training. After graduating
from Berean Academy in Elbing,
Kansas, she earned a B.A. in International
Ministries from Moody Bible
Institute in downtown Chicago. Her
adventures in Haiti began three years
after she and Jarod, also a Moody
grad, got married. They lived and
worked in Port-au-Prince and then Cap Haitian, Haiti from 2002-
2010. When their children's nine-year adoption process came to
a close after the 2010 earthquake, they re-planted their family in
sunny South Florida. Jennifer's primary ministry is to her husband
and five children. She also life coaches and writes regularly
at jenniferebenhack.com, thebettermom.com, club31women.
com, and faithgirlz.com.

Made in the USA
San Bernardino, CA
18 December 2016